Take Our Advice:

A Handbook for Gardening in Northern Virginia

Margaret Fisher & Friends

www.takeouradvice.org
takeouradvice@takeouradvice.org

Library of Congress Control Number: 2012900485

ISBN 978-0-9850090-0-7

SAN 920-2331

Fisher, Margaret
Take Our Advice: A Handbook for Gardening in Northern Virginia

Cover by Karin Fisher

Printed in the United States of America

Our contributors

Life is a group effort, and this book is a great example. All the people below contributed to this book, providing tips, lengthy gardening advice, art work, fact checking and editing. My family also did all those things plus provided the technical assistance that is crucial for publishing. I did the research, a few drawings and the final writing.

My heartfelt thanks to Miriam, for your expertise and for converting me into a gardening fanatic; to Kay, for pointing me firmly towards natives; to Karin, for creating the cover; to Margaret R., for revealing herself as an artist and for devoting many days to hard editing; to Papa and Elaine, for help with publishing; to George, for setting up our web site; to Stuart, for moral support. Thank you, Jon and Joshua, for editing, helping with research, following me all over Northern Virginia to look at nurseries and gardens, doing the heavy gardening and computer work, and just basically putting up with months of conversation dominated by one topic.

And thank you so much, all you gardeners and naturalists who contributed ideas, all those who allowed me to interview you at great length, and all those who helped with the writing itself.

Tom Attanaro
Mary Blanchette
Claire Brown
Ray Burmester
Betty Butterfield
Joan Crump
Bert Curtis
Jeanne Daussin

Nancy Davis
Claudia Donovan
Ellen Egan
Jeanne Fairfax
Kay Fowler
George Ross Fisher, III
George Ross Fisher, IV
Karin Fisher

Susan Gunnerson
Michael Halle
June Hwu
Frank Jencks
Lois Kabat
Janet and Charles Kawecki
Susan Lange
Barbara MacDonald
Emma May
Patsy McCarthy
Terence McCormally,
Judy McDonald
Jim McGlone
Abdel Medina
Mala Mehta
Blythe Merritt
Donna Murphy
Paul Murphy
Ann Marie Newman
Erik Oberg
David Page

Shannon Page
Socorrito Baez-Page
Holly Perlick
Margaret Rogers
Lois Rose
Jonathan Rosenthal
Joshua Rosenthal
Gordon Rothrock
Suzer Sachs
Madeleine Schaefer
Miriam Fisher Schaefer
Kim Scudera
Beatrice Sito
Bob Sjogren
Keith Tomlinson
Julie Wessling
Nancy Wethe
Lynn Witwer
Jody Ziemer
Bob at Burke Nursery
Bonnie at Heather Hill Nursery

Illustrations:

Karin Fisher: Cover
Miriam Fisher Schaefer: Birdbath
Madeleine Schaefer: Hyacinth
Margaret Rogers: Cucumber, daffodil, dogwood, fuchsia, holly, magnolia, pansy, poison ivy, rosemary, tomato, tulip
Margaret Fisher: Balloon flower, bee balm, columbine, oriental bittersweet, photo on back cover

Contents

Neighbors helping neighbors

Have you ever seen a fundraiser cookbook made up of donated recipes? Well, this is a gardening book made up of donated gardening tips. Almost everyone I told about this project said, "I probably can't help because I am no great gardener." But in fact, every single person turned out to have at least one ingenious tip that no one else had mentioned. We all discover things we wish we had known when we first started out, and by sharing those ideas here, we hope to let other people skip some of the trial and error stages of becoming a successful gardener.

A large part of this book is a compilation of our contributors' favorite discoveries, cross checked to the best of my ability. I supplemented this with as much specific information relevant to gardeners in Northern Virginia as I could find. (I apologize for anything I inadvertently left out.) The rest of the book explores some of the basics of gardening in general.

It is easy to find opinions on every gardening subject (much of it contradictory) but difficult to determine whether there is any science behind them. It is also amazing to discover how many different pronouncements there are out there about growing conditions for individual plant species. In the charts, I have included the range of what is mentioned by various authors of gardening books and web sites. However, if a plant reportedly can grow in full sun, part shade and shade, most likely it will do better in one location than another. For example, day lilies will grow just fine in the shade, but they are unlikely to produce flowers without more sun. Hostas will tolerate drought conditions in the shade but get pretty anemic in full sun.

The plant charts are arranged alphabetically by scientific names. The most convenient way to look a plant up by common name is to use the index. Our web site includes a downloadable and sortable table of all the plants mentioned in this book: www.takeouradvice.org.

Just as a garden can never be finished, so there is no end to what could be included in a gardening book. The more you learn, the more you see there is to learn. If there is enough interest, we can put out an updated edition. Meanwhile, any other ideas anyone would like to contribute would be very welcome on our Facebook page.

All the proceeds from sales of this book will be donated to the Student Peace Awards of Fairfax County. If proceeds exceed the needs of the Peace Awards, they will be donated to another similar charity.

Six things beginners should know

1. If you have deer, their presence will dominate your life as a gardener. Either fence them out or learn about deer resistant plants. And remember that "deer resistant" can be a very optimistic term.

2. Indulge your impulse-shopping in annuals, but do a little research before you make a long term commitment to a perennial. A couple minutes spent in reading can save you a lot of grief later. It will take more than just a plant's tag to tell you whether it is suited for your garden. The compact shrub you remember from your childhood may now come in five different sizes and ten different colors.

3. Use soaker hoses. If you plant things that need a lot of watering in our climate (you could avoid that, though - see later sections), you don't want to have to stand there with your hose or to waste water with a sprinkler. Instead, buy a long soaker hose and some metal hairpin-shaped pins. Lay the hose in your garden bed in an S shaped pattern, and then cover it with mulch.

4. Keep track of what you plant. Don't think you will remember (you won't) or that you won't care about the exact botanical and cultivar names (you will). See later chapters for suggestions on how, and start doing this right from the beginning.

5. Feed your plants! Plants need nutrients as much as you do. A flower that is stuck into unimproved clay is not going to be very happy. The best way to do this is to amend your soil with organic materials, but if necessary you can use slow release fertilizer to greatly increase your yield of flowers and vegetables.

6. Mulch! Not only does mulch instantly dress up your garden, it offers essential cooling for the soil and reduces water loss. You can make your own or bring it in, but don't skimp on it.

Hyacinth

What's different about Northern Virginia?

This is a great place to garden, with generally cooperative weather and a plethora of excellent garden centers and other gardening resources.

Weather

Northern Virginia is blessed with a consistently long and delightful growing season. The stretched out season means that perennials that bloom simultaneously up north, bloom in succession here. But within that long stretch, there can be a lot of unpredictability from year to year. On average, this is what to expect:

Winter: After a slow start to winter, temperatures vacillate most of the season around 32 degrees, which is great for creating black ice and causing plants to heave, and for creating ice storms that do some tree damage. Early warm spells sometimes prompt buds, which then get nipped when winter reasserts itself. No matter what the groundhog announces on February 2, spring never comes before March 21. Two or three decent snowfalls per year are average, usually beginning after Christmas, but some years bring next to none and others may bring blizzards.

Spring: Plenty of rain is usual in the spring. March brings spring bulbs; April brings blossoming trees and garden center sales that tempt us to buy annuals too early. Try to resist. Some years have a typical, gradually warming spring; others leap from winter to summer within the space of a week, with hot temperatures starting as early as April.

Summer: Planting mostly comes to a halt by mid to late June, with humid, eighty and ninety degree weather that persists into August most years and sometimes beyond. Rain comes in the form of thunderstorms, which sometimes deliver less precipitation than it seems; supplemental watering is often needed for new plantings. At some point, most summers bring a period of extended drought, sending the lawn into dormancy. It greens up again when the rains return.

Fall: Hurricanes and cooler weather bring steadier rains again, typically in late September. A beautiful, lingering fall follows - an excellent time for planting which can continue almost to Thanksgiving or even beyond.

Some spectacular plants thrive in this environment as if they were made for it, for the simple reason that they were. Plants native to the Chesapeake watershed as a rule are accustomed to summer droughts, repeated winter thaws, *etc.,* and require a minimum of care once established.

First frost free day (meaning the last frost of the spring)
Average: April 23 (rarely later than May 9 or earlier than April 6) (Dulles airport)

Last frost free day
Average: October 13 (rarely earlier than September 29 or later than October 26) (Dulles airport)

Average precipitation
40-45 inches per year, distributed fairly evenly, with May being on average slightly wetter, and December through February somewhat drier than the other months.

USDA Hardiness Zone 7a

"Hardiness Zones" refer only to average minimum temperatures. Zone 7 is 0-10 degrees Fahrenheit, and the "a" means that it is more like the lower end of that range. The zone system does not take into account the summer heat, precipitation, altitude, or other factors, so just because a plant grows somewhere in 7a, it does not mean it will necessarily grow well here.

Sun

It's pretty brutal for much of the growing season, even quite late in the afternoon. Western exposures really bake.

Soil

The much maligned Virginia clay is not actually a bad thing. It provides structure to the soil which keeps your plants from falling over. Undisturbed woodland has a thick layer of humus on top of the bed of clay. Unfortunately, that topsoil is often scraped away in the construction process, leaving solid clay that needs to be amended before planting. A charming difference between digging holes here compared to up north is that your shovel will not go "clink" on a rock when you stick it in the ground.

Bugs

Bugs are also not bad things. They are of course essential for the survival of plants, animals and humans. But they do need to be taken into account, as there are many more here than in a more northern climate.

Critters

Voles, rabbits and groundhogs can trip up the unsuspecting gardener, but if you live in a deer area, you will need some very serious strategizing if you want any garden at all. If you are feeling sorry for them, feel more sorry for all the other animals whose food sources are stripped away by an overpopulation of deer that do significant damage to our natural ecosystem.

Homesick?

Many of us are transplants from other parts of the country or from abroad. We often long to recreate the gardens of our original homes. Don't set yourself up for disappointment. The climate here supports a great deal of plant diversity, but that does not include tropical or desert plants.

Handy tips

Plant what your neighbors plant
What you see growing is what grows here.

But don't plant alien invasives!
A lot of what you see is imported ornamentals that are taking over and destroying our local environment. See the list of what not to buy, and think about specializing in plants that are native to this region.

Emulate success
If you live in a development, chances are someone has already planted the type of shrub you are planning to buy. Take a look at which side of the house it is flourishing and follow the example.

Plant odd numbers
One plant is an interesting specimen. Three make at least a mini mass planting. But even numbers are tricky: if you aim for symmetry but don't quite get there because of the vicissitudes of plant growth, the result is apt to look dumb.

Decide
When you go to the garden center and are bowled over by the choices - unable to choose between all the beautiful colors available for one species - make yourself choose! Repeating the same color throughout your garden ties it together. Multiple random colors are tricky to blend nicely.

Or... don't decide!
Some people are designers, others are collectors. But don't expect your garden to look like Versailles if you buy everything in sight.

Perennials are your friends
Why pay for new plants and go to all that trouble to plant every year, when you could plant once instead? Perennials have shorter bloom times than annuals and are more expensive up front, but in the long run, they allow you to develop a much more interesting garden with a much lower water requirement. Use annuals as temporary fillers and as container plants.

Foliage is your other friend
Flowers come and go, but different shapes and shades of foliage make the garden interesting throughout the season. And if you live in deer country, cultivating a preference for the color green will save you a lot of disappointment.

If a plant does not belong where it is, take it out
You pull up weeds, don't you? It is possible to live a life of nonviolence and still remove unwanted plants! You may be able to find a new home for some things, but others may need to live on as compost.

Accept your losses and move on
If a plant did not work, don't keep trying it.

Prune most shrubs immediately after flowering
Generally speaking, next year's flowers start to form shortly after this year's flowers fade. You therefore have quite a short window of opportunity to prune. There are a few exceptions which bloom on new growth and which therefore should be pruned early in the season, such as tea roses and certain types of hydrangeas.

Think drought

Succulents are good to grow as they do not require much water. There are many different perennial succulents available which add variety to the garden when mixed in with other plants. Some grow tall; others stay close to the ground and can make great ground covers.

Trees grow

If the front of your house is in full sun and there are no trees nearby, it will always be in full sun. But full sun at the edge of the woods will be shade in a few years, so plan accordingly. If a plant no longer produces blooms, perhaps conditions changed since it was planted. Be prepared to move things.

Early shoppers may get fooled

The flowers of some plants open in the morning and are closed up by evening, making a very disappointing display for most commuters. Examples include morning glory (which are invasive anyway), portulaca (which only flowers in bright sun), and spiderwort.

Find the right spot

Within your garden are many microclimates, depending on the shade, soil, wind and drainage. If a plant is not flourishing in one location, it might do just fine a few feet over

Save time - plant bulbs

Bulbs are easy to plant and grow and add interesting shapes to your garden. Examples of summer bulbs that work around here include caladiums, oriental lilies, allium, gladiolus, dahlias and crocosmia. Of these, though, only the oriental lilies and allium will reliably make it through our winter, unless you dig them up. If you don't feel like digging, you may simply use them the way you do annuals and replace them the next year. Although there will be some attrition from being eaten by animals, many spring bulbs (daffodils, crocuses, snowdrops, hyacinths, scilla, glory-of-the-snow) will come back year after year.

However, tulips usually do not make it in this climate - the bulbs tend to rot – so resign yourself to replanting every fall.

Some like wet feet
Some plants have to be planted in wet soil. Examples include *Lobelia cardinalis*, ligularia and hardy hibiscus.

Eliminate lawn the easy way
Cut the grass as low as possible. Cover with 6 layers of newspaper then three inches of mulch. Leave it a couple months, and then plant away.

Reuse, but don't recycle plastic plant pots
Unfortunately, with rare exceptions, garden centers are unable to reuse the pots in which plants are sold. Seedlings are very prone to fungal diseases; the growers therefore must use sterile containers. Some nurseries might be able to use a few for repotting or growing plants on site. Waste Management, the company that recycles plastic from Northern Virginia, is also unable to take the pots, because the dirt and rocks would contaminate their bales of plastic, potentially leading to whole loads being thrown into the trash.

Take advantage of fall
Fall is an excellent time to plant. Your plants will have many months to establish roots before they get hit by the summer heat and drought. The roots actually keep growing for a while, even after the leaves fall off.

"Fall" does not mean September
September around here is still full summer, with plenty of heat and drought potential. Labor Day is a good time for planting and for spreading grass seed up north, but around here you should wait another few weeks.

Foil the squirrels

To prevent squirrels from digging up your bulbs, place a moth ball on the ground on top. Alternatively, encase the bulbs in a little chicken wire cage, or cover the whole area with chicken wire under a layer of dirt of mulch. Iris tubers are particularly vulnerable to squirrels, because they have to be planted very shallow. Instead, you can buy the iris in a pot already sprouted, which will give it a chance to get established; the squirrels leave them alone after that. The same is true for bulbs such as hyacinths, (though the squirrels may dig them up in a future year).

Choose the right rake

Use a wire rake in the beds and a bamboo rake on the grass. This way you minimize the mulch you dig up in the beds and the grass you dig up in the lawn.

Save work while weeding

Use a small bucket for yard maintenance, then empty the bucket into a leaf bag when it is full. This way you don't have to constantly stand up to reach into the bag.

Kill driveway weeds naturally

Pour vinegar onto weeds that are on the sidewalk or driveway to kill them. Do not do this in the beds because it will also kill surrounding plants.

Fertilizer can help compensate for insufficient sun

A common example of this is lush lawns growing in partial shade. Since turf grass prefers full sun, landscaping companies spread a lot of fertilizer. This many chemicals is bad for the Chesapeake watershed, but it illustrates that you may be able to coax your plants in the shade into greater lushness by enriching the soil. Better, of course, is to pick plants that are suited for the location.

Don't expect a finished product
A garden is never finished. It is okay to plant now for now, and space things close together even though they will need more room when they reach their final size. You can always move (or remove) things later.

Pansy

Favorite tools and equipment

Keep your tools where you use them. Right next to the door is a good place for your gloves and pruners, and perhaps a pocket knife to carry with you everywhere. Finding a place in your garden to keep other frequently used tools will save you a lot of aggravation and trips to your garage.

Everyone can suggest a favorite tool. But the surprise winner in the Best Tools category is...the humble

Pitchfork!
This is the best tool for heaving mulch and turning compost heaps. It is much easier than a shovel for getting a good amount in one scoop and is much easier on the back.

Here are the runner ups:

Two pairs of gloves
Get the stretchy kind with nitrile coating for ordinary gardening and leather ones with long sleeves for heavy work, thorns or anywhere where you might run across poison ivy. Don't settle for the first ones you see: gloves come in different sizes, styles and materials, and some are far more comfortable than others.

Waterproof shoes
Soggy sneakers and socks are a major disincentive for gardening in the early morning dew or after a rain. The Muck Boot Company makes

rubber shoes and boots with a soft lining, available on line. They are great for walking the dog in the rain, too.

Gardening seats
For those with bad backs or knees, a small stool or folding chair is helpful when weeding. You can buy a strong, stable type of stool for gardening which will not skitter away on wheels when you sit and which provides good support. Carry a bucket or large pot to throw weeds into.

Kneeling pad
It is more comfortable to kneel than to bend over or squat for long pe-riods.

Hand truck
A small, inexpensive dolly is much more stable and easier to maneuver than a wheelbarrow. One of our contributors actually broke her arm as she tried to wrangle an uncooperative wheelbarrow! You can use a dolly to move heavy bags and trash cans around. (A big garbage can is a good container for mixing soil.) Buy a dolly with solid wheels so you never have to inflate a flat tire again.

Solid wheels for your wheelbarrow
If you do have to use one, replace the pneumatic tire with a solid wheel.

A good shovel
It is surprising how much easier it is to dig a hole with a good, strong, sharp shovel. Get the kind that is slightly pointy with a serrated border to make it easier to cut through roots.

Pickax
For digging through solid clay or rocky soil, a pickax is faster than a shovel.

Good quality pruners
It is worth looking on line to read about the relative merits of various brands of pruners. A high quality tool can make a big difference if you do much pruning. Felco 2, for example, are excellent pruners, available with replacement blades.

Ratchet pruners
Ratchet pruners such as Fisker's makes it possible to cut through thicker, tougher branches.

Long-handled pruning hook with an attached saw
If you are buying a tree pruner anyway, get one with a saw.

Trademark Tools 75-1079 Hawk Deluxe Multi Function Garden Scissors
This extremely handy tool combines a folding pruner with a little knife, saw and weeder that fits in your pocket.

Electric hedge trimmers
Electric pruners make quick work out of cutting back ornamental grass and liriope in the late winter, not to mention hedges.

Holsters
Carry your pruner on a belt holster. This is much easier than having to lug around a full belt of tools.

Small seed sowers
A hand-held contraption allows you to adjust the opening according to the size of the seeds and plant small seeds much more uniformly than by hand. They are quite inexpensive.

Japanese weeder
The triangular blade on this hand tool makes weeding go much more quickly.

Garden weasel cultivator
The spiked wheels on this tool dig up weeds and cut their roots. This performs really well in a garden in which the ground has already been worked (as opposed to a new bed).

Rototillers
A rototiller is a big help to anyone doing major vegetable gardening. These can be rented or purchased.

Mantis tiller
Mantis makes a very light, two cycle small tiller that allows you to weed and till between vegetable rows. Our reviewer says, "I don't know how I did a garden without it!" It is totally different from a big tiller which you use once or twice a year to turn the entire garden under.

Electric weed whackers
Although it is a pain to drag the extension cord around your yard, electric weed whackers are dependable and light weight. Gas powered ones are very heavy and require strong arms to start. The rechargeable ones tend to break after a season or two and have too small a cutting radius, which slows down the work.

Mulching mowers
If you are in the market for a new lawn mower, get the mulching kind. Rather than blowing the large grass clippings into a bag, this kind of mower cuts it up fine and leaves it on the ground, where it returns the nutrients to the soil. You can take several passes over your fall leaves to grind them up in place rather than raking them.

Drop cloth
A big tarp, sheet or drop cloth is the easiest way to move leaves when you are raking. Rake them onto the cloth, fold the corners together, then drag it behind.

Pop-up yard waste bin
These very light bins spring open to make a very nice container for moving yard waste.

Green stretchy tape
This is a cheap and satisfactory material for tying things up.

Cheap stakes
Hardware stores sell 12 foot thin strips of wood called "furring strips" for under a dollar apiece. Cut them on the diagonal to make nice stakes. As the ends rot, cut them a little shorter. You can use the really short pieces as plant markers.

Bright halogen light
For those of us who rush home late from work and dash out to work like mad in the fading light, there is a possible solution: put up a very bright light.

Self-watering hanging planters
Flowering annuals suck up tremendous amounts of water in really hot weather. A "self-watering" container has a reservoir at the bottom, so you can get away with skipping a day or two of watering in all but the hottest weather.

Soil testers
Measuring pH can help you decide which plants are suitable and what soil amendments are needed for shrubs or lawn. Unfortunately, the inexpensive pH and moisture meters may or may not actually work. A pH kit is your best bet for reliability.

Sunscreen and hats
A lifetime of gardening need not lead to wrinkles, brown spots and skin cancer. Cover up. Bug spray is a good idea, too.

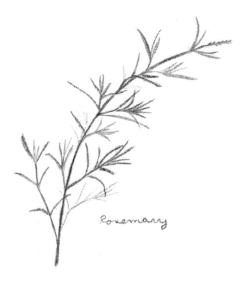

Rosemary

Sadder but wiser

Our contributors would like to spare you the aggravation of some very common mistakes.

Choosing your plants

Pick the right size
Plants come in different sizes! Don't buy one unless you know what its ultimate size will be. Azaleas for instance, may vary from miniature to huge.

Avoid impulse shopping
It is almost impossible to resist the many amazing plants in the garden center, but we all lose a lot of plants for lack of some advance research. Pay attention to sun and moisture requirements, and also to whether a given species is prone to fungi and insect damage.

Trust, but verify
The helpful and knowledgeable people at the garden center cannot possibly keep every detail of hundreds of plants in their heads. Nothing is as aggravating as spending seventy dollars on a shrub, only to discover that it requires a flood plain and all you have is desert. Before you actually pay for a plant that you think will fit your needs, look it up in a plant book (many garden centers have reference books) or else check it on your smart phone.

GardenPilot is a wonderful app for iPhone which includes plant information for 15,000 plants. The Droid users among us can't wait to have someone invent the equivalent for us.

Always go by the scientific name
In your conversations with garden center staff, you may both assume that you each know what the other means by a common name. But if you do not double check the Latin name, you may find yourself buying the wrong plant altogether.

Don't be fooled by blooms
Rumor has it that some garden centers fertilize heavily, resulting in gorgeous flowers on display. When you get them home and remove them from their rich diet, they may not do so well.

Don't plant too early
You can buy annuals in early April, but try to resist. We could have frost as late as early May. Perennials can be put in much earlier, though.

Avoid certain plants altogether

When they say aggressive, they really mean it
Think long and hard before planting anything that is called "aggressive." Some, such as bee balm and lamb's ears, can be easily pulled up and contained. Others will become a permanent infestation. For example, *Ajuga* spreads by self-seeding. You may be tempted to enjoy its beautiful purple flowers that spring up in your lawn, but before you know it, you will have a big patch of broad leaves instead of grass. Another example is mint, which forms an impenetrable mat of stolons (spreading shoots) that is very difficult to pull up. Keep mint in a pot, either as a container plant, or sunk into your garden.

Don't let delphiniums tempt you
Many a delphinium has met a sad death in our gardens. This is definitely a flower for experts only, especially in this hot climate.

Don't plant morning glory
It is easily grown from seed and climbs your fence in a gratifying way the first year, but forever after that, it sprouts up all over your garden and makes a tangle. Plus, it only blooms in the morning and is an invasive plant in Virginia.

Beware of fringe flowers
This woody shrub does not do well under snow. The weight shears off branches which won't grow back.

Watch out for thirsty plants
Oak and tulip poplar tree roots will suck the water right out of your garden.

Some plants are just expensive deer food
If you are unsure if a plant is deer resistant, just put in one the first year and watch to see what happens.

Location, location, location

Watch what you put next to your house
Some plants are a nuisance if planted too close to your house. Peonies attract ants and form a nice ant ladder into your kitchen. Crepe myrtles shed a lot: first flower petals, then their leaves, then hard little pellets which can clog up your gutters (plus they are becoming invasive in Virginia anyway).

Pumpkins are fun
But don't plant a pumpkin or a squash in your flower garden. It will take over everything.

Look up
If you plant a tree under a power line, eventually you will have a decapitated half tree, thanks to the power company, which has right of way. The power company does not like evergreen trees in their easement and might remove them altogether. The big trucks need access, so don't get too fond of your other plantings, either.

Prune very carefully

Don't prune hydrangea stems
The new blooms grow on the woody stems.

Don't prune roses too low
Since many roses are grafted onto the roots of another kind of rose, if you prune too low to the ground, what comes up will not be the hybrid you expected but another type altogether.

Don't prune woody herbs too low or too early (or maybe at all)
Certain herbs - lavender, thyme, sage and rosemary - are woody plants. Just like trees, if you cut them down, they die. Pruning one too low is likely to kill the plant or injure it severely.

Raised beds

Raise them higher
Six inches high is insufficient for a raised bed. The roots of one plant will be crowding its neighbor. Root crops and corn espe-

cially need more depth. Spend a little more and make the beds twelve inches deep from the start.

Wood rots

Plain pine boards have a natural appeal, but you will eventually regret using them to build a raised bed. Pick something more durable.

Don't waste your money

Don't be fooled

Expensive garden aids that look so intriguing in catalogs are rarely worth the money.

An idea whose time has not yet come

Those adorable solar-powered lights and fountains you see for sale in catalogs end up creating a big messy carbon footprint, as they quickly break and go off in the garbage truck.

Don't let your tomatoes water themselves

Self-watering planters are a disaster for tomato plants. Too much of a good thing, apparently.

Upside down tomato planters don't work

Don't even bother.

Be careful with containers without drainage holes

A couple days of rain will make a sodden mess out of the soil in even a large container with no drainage hole, rotting the roots of your plants. If you already have a pot like that, drill a hole if possible, or use a container within the container, raised up off the bottom.

Miscellaneous

Fend off the deer
Strawberries set their blossoms in the fall. If you want fruit the next year, don't let the deer nibble on them during that period.

Watch the pH
Some plants, such as blueberries, absolutely require you to adjust the pH of the soil. If you don't, they do poorly or even die.

Watch out for imitators
If you allow your dog to watch you digging in the garden, it might just decide to help you out.

Protect electric cords
When using a chainsaw or hedge clipper, put the extension cord over your shoulder or wrap it around your waist to prevent cutting the cord. Don't use an electric lawn mower when it is growing dark outside.

Mulching is not a substitute for weeding
Weed first.

Watch where you put your mulch
It is not a good idea to dump a truck full of mulch on your driveway, at least not if you plan to drive on it that summer. Don't dump it on grass either, because it is very difficult to remove completely. For small quantities, you could use a tarp which you can slide around the yard.

Bugs need to eat, too
As do rabbits, squirrels, mold... Vegetable gardening in this climate is harder than it looks. You can be casual with flowers, but do some research before planting vegetables.

There is a reason why people buy garden packs
Growing from seeds is also a lot harder than it looks. Starting indoors is messy and difficult. Most of the seeds will not turn into anything unless you have the right temperature, humidity, air circulation and lighting. Starting flowers outside from seeds after the last frost has similar low yields and will delay your viewing (or eating) pleasure quite a lot. It's a good thing that the packages include a lot of seeds, since only a small percentage will ever germinate. If you invest the time it takes to learn how to plant seeds correctly, though, it can be fun.

Tulip

Know what you have

You many think you will remember the names of your plants, but you won't. Then when you try to buy another matching plant or recommend one to a friend, you'll be in trouble. A simple and popular strategy is to just keep all the tags in a pot or a bag so you can find them when you need them. A slightly more organized approach is to keep a running list of the plants you purchase, with their scientific as well as common names. For the Über Organized, you could make a spreadsheet, which would allow you to resort the list in a variety of ways (you could start by downloading the table from our web site and add columns for planting dates, locations, *etc.* www.takeouradvice.org)

You may also think you won't need to know the scientific name, but you will. Many plants have multiple common names, and many common names refer to multiple plant genera. For example, the type of *Caladium* known as "elephant ear" is also known as "heart of Jesus" and "angel wings." And the term "elephant ear" is used to refer to not only *Caladiums* but also the genera *Alocasia, Colocasia,* and *Xanthosoma.*

What's in a name?

Scientific names are always in italics and have two parts, although one might be abbreviated. The first part, always capitalized, is the genus. When you add the second part, the resulting two-part name is the species (spp.). For example, Cornus florida (or *C. florida*) is the flowering dogwood.

Subspecies (ssp. or subsp.) are different races within a species. For example, *Cornus florida* ssp. *florida* is the Virginia state tree.

Varieties (v. or var.) are naturally occurring strains that are too similar to be considered different subspecies. For example, *Cornus florida* var. *rubra* is the pink flowering dogwood.

Cultivars are varieties that were selected by humans to breed true. The name is not italicized and is enclosed in single quotation marks. For instance, *Cornus florida* 'Appalachian Spring' is resistant to dogwood anthracnose, a fungus that has been killing off our state tree.

Hybrids are a cross between two species, indicated with an X, and can occur either naturally or by human intervention. For example, *Cornus × rutgersensis* is a cross between *Cornus florida* and *Cornus kousa,* the Japanese dogwood.

Clones are genetically identical offspring. Plants clone themselves when they send out shoots that grow into new plants. Mass cloning engineered by humans is risky since lack of genetic diversity can lead to disaster when diseases strike.

Label your Plants

Having a clear label on your plants will make you feel very professional. More practically, knowing which plant is where is useful, especially in the spring as things start to emerge. Invest in metal plant markers: the wooden ones rot away quickly and the plastic ones break. You can make an impression with a ball point pen on copper labels, then go over them with a marker. A battery operated labeling machine is very helpful (such as the Brother P-touch GL100 model sold by Gardener's Supply Company and some garden centers). The printed labels are easy to read and waterproof.

Plant tags are very nice. The types that hang on trees and shrubs are satisfactory. But the ones in the ground tend to disappear eventually under the growing plant or leaves, or by being raked up. So keeping a list or making a diagram showing which perennials are in which garden bed is a good idea. If you like computers, you can use the drawing function to make a color coded map, using a key for the plant names. Or more simply, you can create a table in a document, with each column representing one of your garden rows. Professionals use garden designing software, some of which can be downloaded for free.

For vegetables, you need to keep track of when you planted, sprayed, fertilized, and pruned. One way to do that, for plants that need staking, would be to write the information, as well as the plant name, on its tall wooden stake.

Keeping a journal

A garden journal is not a necessity, but it is fun. You can buy pretty books for this purpose. More flexible, though, is a loose leaf binder with any of the following sections.

> *Precipitation chart*
>> Recording rainfall with a rain gauge is important. If the total is less than an inch in a week, you may need to do some watering, especially for new plantings. (Don't try to use a glass rain gauge when the temperature is below freezing. The glass will break!)

> *Planting diagrams*

> *To Do list*
>> Remind yourself to prune your roses on St. Patrick's Day or to transplant a tall plant to the rear in the fall.

Journal

Jot down notable events, success and failures for the season. It is fun to look back on what happened in previous years.

Individual plant records

Mail order company contact information

Vegetable timing records

Plant guarantees

Pocket dividers

Store receipts, seed packets, *etc.*

Week-by-week bloom record

If you keep track of what was blooming in a given week (though this varies some from year to year), you can get a rough idea of which plants will go well together.

Clear plastic sheet protectors for photographs

You can buy a pre-packaged version of the above from HoJo Publications. www.agardenersjournal.com

Precipitation chart

Year 20__

	Jan	Feb	Mar	Apr	May	Jun	Jul	Aug	Sep	Oct	Nov	Dec
1												
2												
3												
4												
5												
6												
7												
8												
9												
10												
11												
12												
13												
14												
15												
16												
17												
18												
19												
20												
21												
22												
23												
24												
25												
26												
27												
28												
29												
30												
31												
Total												

Plant Records

Common name:
Scientific name:
Sun requirement:
Height:
Width:
Comments:

Date purchased:
Place of purchase:
Price:
Quantity:
Location planted:

Plant tag or picture:

Common name:
Scientific name:
Sun requirement:
Height:
Width:
Comments:

Date purchased:
Place of purchase:
Price:
Quantity:
Location planted:

Plant tag or picture:

Common name:
Scientific name:
Sun requirement:
Height:
Width:
Comments:

Date purchased:
Place of purchase:
Price:
Quantity:
Location planted:

Plant tag or picture:

What does "full sun" actually mean?

Measuring the sun exposure of your garden before you start is crucial. You cannot grow a meadow in a forest clearing or power line ease-ment, for instance, as the tall surrounding trees will block the sun for much of the day.

There is some fuzziness of the definitions for the various sun exposure terms that you may read or find on plant labels. "Full sun" definitely means at least six hours per day, but some plants such as vegetables really need eight to ten hours per day.

"Partial sun" or "partial shade" means that the plant needs 3-6 hours of direct sun per day. The terms sometimes are used interchangeably. However, being shaded in the morning is not the same as being shaded from the scorching afternoon sun. "Partial sun" usually implies that the plant needs more sun and is more heat tolerant. "Partial shade" implies that the plant should be protected from the sun during the afternoon.

"Shade" does not mean pitch black, of course. More plants tolerate dappled shade than can live in really deep shade.

Regardless of a plant's label, how much sun it needs or will tolerate var-ies with the strength of the sun and on how much you water.

If you methodically plot out the sun exposure in different parts of your garden, you may be in for some surprises. What is baking hot at noon may really be dappled shade the rest of the day. What is dappled sun in

April may be full shade in July, when the shrubs need light to produce next year's flowers. So create a chart such as the one below once the trees have leafed out and make hourly observations.

	7 am	8	9	10	11	noon	1	2	3	4	5 pm
front door	●	●	◐	◐	○	○	○	◐	◐	●	●
east end back garden	●	●	●	●	◐	○	○	○	○	○	○
middle	●	◐	○	○	○	○	○	○	○	◐	●
west end	◐	○	○	○	○	○	○	◐	●	●	●

What is in all those mysterious bags and boxes?

Are you bewildered by those huge piles of heavy plastic bags and shelf after shelf of boxes at the gardening center? Here is how you decide which ones you need.

Mulch
See the separate section on this topic.

Topsoil
"Topsoil" just refers to unimproved soil. Its advantage is its lower price. It has organic material in it but also some mix of minerals such as clay, silt, sand, *etc*. When putting in a new bed, you start with topsoil (either store-bought or what is in the ground already) and add soil amendments.

Soil Amendments
The goals of amendments are to
- Add nutrients
- Create air spaces for the roots to grow ("lighten" the soil)
- Hold moisture
- Increase drainage
- Change the pH

Examples include:

- *Compost* This is partially decomposed material that lightens the soil and provides nutrients. You can make this yourself from leaves, yard waste and kitchen scraps (see chapter on composting), or you can buy it in a bag. Commercial compost products contain a wide variety of ingredients, which should be listed on the label. Those include leaves, manure (cow, horse, poultry), bedding straw, cocoa hulls, corn cobs, sludge, wood, paper, cardboard, lobster and crab shells, feather meal, alfalfa meal, cottonseed meal, *etc.* Since different plants need different quantities of nutrients, there could be something to be said for putting a variety of materials into your compost.
- *Leaf mold* This is simply ground up leaves that have been composted. Adding this to your soil improves water retention and soil structure, though it adds limited amounts of nutrients. It is easy to make your own.
- *Humus* This is a totally confusing term, as the scientific use of the word is unrelated to what is sold in bags. For gardening center purposes, humus is the same as compost. Read the label. If the label does not list the ingredients on a bag of humus or compost, most likely it is made from leaf mold which the company got from the county and bagged up.
- *Peat moss* Usually made from Canadian sphagnum moss, peat moss adds moisture retention and air to the soil, though it provides very little in the way of nutrients. It is the least expensive soil lightener available in bags. It is very acidic. Warning: the harvesting of peat bogs damages an important ecosystem. There are many alternatives for improving your garden soil. Alternatives for potting mix also exist, but some may be harder to locate. These include coir (made from coconut husks), rice hulls, alfalfa and leaf mold compost.
- *Peat humus* Composted peat moss.
- *Super fine* Finely ground mulch adds organic material and lightens the soil.

- *Compost tea* A liquid made from steeping compost in water for a few days.
- *Moisture crystals* These clever little polymers plump up amazingly and then release their water slowly. There is a great deal of doubt, though, whether they actually do a good job at giving up that moisture to the plants, possibly binding it instead.
- *Lime, dolomite* Raises the pH (thus making it more basic and less acidic). Often used for lawns. Provides calcium.
- *Sulfur* Acidifies the soil (and turns hydrangeas blue). Slow acting, so plan far ahead.
- *Iron sulfate* Acidifies the soil. Fast acting. Iron deficiency causes yellowing. Applying iron to the lawn makes it turn a darker green.
- *Aluminum sulfate* Also acidifies the soil, but caution is advised because too much aluminum is toxic to roots. Fast acting.
- *Perlite, vermiculite* These minerals lighten the soil and improve drainage. Perlite is the little white stuff you find in potting mixes and is made by heating volcanic glass.
- *Gypsum* Loosens clay soil.
- *Wetting agents (surfactants)* By dissolving the waxy coating on organic material the same way detergent does, surfactants keep the water from beading and rolling off. They are dangerous to aquatic creatures and need to be kept out of waterways.

All of the above break down over time, which is why you might sometimes include
- *Teeny little rocks* These come under a variety of trade names and permanently lighten and improve the moisture retention of soil. They may be made of slate or of a ceramic material.
- *Sand* Lightens the soil and improves drainage. Use coarse builder's sand for this purpose, not fine sand.

Fertilizer
- *Chemical fertilizers* contain varying combinations of nitrogen, phosphorus and potassium, which is what the three numbers re-

fer to. Nitrogen promotes rapid growth and especially foliage. (Lawn fertilizer for example could be something like 26-3-2 - very high in nitrogen - as opposed to fertilizer for tomatoes, which would be something like 5-10-5 or 5-10-10, although 10-10-10 will do). Phosphorus promotes root growth, flowers and seeds (speaking very simplistically). Potassium promotes toughness: strong stems, winter hardiness, drought tolerance, disease and pest resistance. The numbers indicate the percentage of the mix; for example, 5-10-15 means that the mixture contains 5% nitrogen, 10% phosphorus and 15% potassium. The material therefore contains a total of 30% fertilizer and 70% filler. (If there were no filler, then the mixture would be too strong and could burn tender plants). It is also possible to buy the ingredients separately; examples are Super Phosphate, Super Nitrate, and potash (potassium). Nitrogen breaks down quickly and needs to be reapplied every year or even more often. Phosphorus and potassium break down much more slowly.

- *Organic fertilizers* contain various ratios of nitrogen, phosphorus, and potassium, plus other secondary elements such as calcium, magnesium, sulfur, zinc and manganese. Most are less concentrated than chemical fertilizers, so much larger quantities are required. Be aware that pets may try to eat some of these products!
    - *Blood meal* (Nitrogen source)
    - *Kelp meal* (Potassium and nitrogen)
    - *Bone meal* (Mostly phosphorus, some nitrogen)
    - *Cottonseed meal* (Soil acidifier, mostly nitrogen, some phosphorus)
    - *Bat guano* (Ratio of ingredients varies, depending on which kind of bat!)
    - *Alfalfa meal* (Approximately 3-1-2)
    - *Fish fertilizer* (Nitrogen and phosphorus)

- o *Various manures* (Balance depends on type. Horse manure is approximately 0.6-0.6-0.4. Fresh chicken manure is 1.5-1.5-0.5, but "Chickity Doo Doo" is 5-3-2.5.)
- o *Worm castings* (Estimates vary from 3-2-2 to 0.5-0.1-0.1, but the nutrients are thought to be more bioavailable than from other sources.)
- o *Shrimp shells* (Shells are made of calcium, which strengthens the stem of any plant and the skin of tomatoes.)
- o *Greensand* (Mined from the ocean floor, greensand contains 3% potassium plus silica, iron, magnesium, lime and many other trace minerals. Also lightens the soil.)

Mycorrhizae spores
These fungi are essential for plant roots to take up needed mineral nutrients. They are present naturally in all soil. However, if the soil has been stripped away to build a house, some gardeners think that it helps to add a little mycorrhizae to the planting mix. Others say it is a waste of money.

Mixes
If you don't want to go to the trouble of making your own combination, you can buy a mix.

- *Planting mix* Read the ingredients label. If it has no label, you will have to decide whether to trust the seller to know what is standard. Most likely leaf mulch is the main ingredient.
- *Potting mix* The challenge of container gardening is to maintain the right moisture level. A well-drained pot will dry out fast. Most commercial potting mixes contain perlite or vermiculite combined with peat moss. The ratio of those two main ingredients determines the consistency and lightness of the mix. Some include other additives, such as limestone, wetting agents, polymer crystals, mycorrhizae or chemical fertilizers. Certain house plants need very particular conditions, hence the need for special mixes for cacti, orchids, *etc.*

Mulch

Mulching your plants keeps the roots cooler and moister and helps retard weeds. As it breaks down, organic mulch becomes a soil amendment. Mulches have been proven to increase plant yields. They are essential around trees planted in lawns, because allowing grass to grow close to the trunk will slow down the tree growth noticeably. Among the organic mulches, which one to choose is mostly a matter of looks and convenience, because the effect on the soil is the same. Garden centers around here sell a lot of hardwood and pine bark mulch because it is locally available, which saves shipping costs. On a slope, pine bark mulch or finely chopped mulch, being lighter, may be more likely to wash away.

Examples of mulch include:
- *Dead leaves* This is the preferred mulch, as you "make it on site" and it works just as well as the kind you bring in. This is how nature solves its mulch needs.
- *Grass clippings*
- *Newspaper*
- *Pine bark (shredded or nuggets)*
- *Hardwood* Lasts longer than pine bark mulch, which also means that it does not amend the soil as quickly.
- *Cedar* Lasts even longer but is more expensive. Cedar wood repels some insects, which may be good or bad, depending on what you are trying to accomplish.

- *Cypress* No better than any other mulch. The harvesting of trees for this purpose is causing serious damage to the cypress swamps.
- *Colored mulch* Depending on the manufacturer, the dyes could be potentially toxic, and the wood could be recycled treated wood that contains arsenic.

The term "mulch" actually applies to anything used to cover the soil and therefore can also refer to inorganic material such as gravel, synthetic material such as landscape cloth and plastic, and even live plants such as turf grass. The results of research studies are clear: coarse, organic mulch does the best job. One and a half inches is enough to conserve water, moderate soil temperatures, add nutrients, and reduce soil compaction and erosion. A four inch layer is needed to prevent weeds. One alternative is to put down 6 sheets of newspaper under a thinner layer of mulch. Contrary to rumor, studies show that wood chip mulch does not attract termites. Landscape cloth and plastic are not nearly as effective as organic mulches and can cause other problems when the roots try to grow into them.

Free mulch and leaf mold
If you take a look at the huge mountains of free mulch that the local counties and cities put out for the taking, you will suddenly understand why landscapers around here pile it on so thickly at every opportunity. You will also wonder why you have ever paid for mulch. Help yourself: just drive up with a pitchfork and a container or heavy duty bag and take it away. If you are using strong plastic bags such as contractor bags, you can hold them open with stiff wire hoops or a trash can. Big trash barrels make very handy containers for transporting mulch if your car is tall enough to accommodate them. (If you transport a great deal of mulch, you may need the more expensive trash cans, as the handles eventually may break off of the cheap kind.)

For those lucky enough to own a pick-up truck or trailer, there is a conveyor belt that will load the mulch for you at the I66 transfer station in Fairfax as well as other sites. If you need a whole lot of mulch but don't have a truck, see the Fairfax County web site for a list of delivery companies. www.fairfaxcounty.gov/dpwes/trash/dispmulch.htm Arlington County has its own delivery service for a small fee www.arlingtonva.us/des or call 703-228-6570.

Mulch is available year round in Fairfax. Leaf mold, which comes from the leaves that are collected by vacuum trucks then ground up, is only available until the fall supplies run out. (The leaves that you leave in bags at the curb are given to the compost company to be re-bagged and sold.) The town of Vienna will deliver leaf mold for free to people living within the town limits.

The free mulch is made from ground up brush that comes from homeowners. Since that could include poison ivy (as could store-bought mulch), it is best to wear gloves when handling it. Weeds are also included, but the gigantic mulch mountains get so hot that weeds are unlikely to survive, although their seeds might. To avoid contributing your own noxious weeds, when you take invasive plants to the transfer station, put them with the trash to be incinerated rather than in the brush pile. When tying up bundles of brush, please use biodegradable string. You can also buy paper yard waste bags so that they can be composted with your leaves.

Compost

Bacteria, water, air and heat work together to create compost, in which the nutrients from the original material become more available for your plants than if you put the materials straight on top of your garden. You could simply do the latter, but don't expect to see very fast results, and orange peels on top of your landscaping are pretty unsightly. You should not dig uncomposted material into your soil, as the breakdown process sucks up nitrogen. If you let your compost decompose long enough, eventually it disappears entirely, just as the nutrients in your garden get washed out over time and need to be replaced.

There are essentially two ways to compost: the "14 day" method and the "1 year" method. If you have the energy and determination, it is possible to convert yard debris into an adequate composted soil conditioner in 2 weeks. Whatever material you choose to compost, such as leaves, must be shredded and moistened. (Unshredded leaves will not compost in 14 days!) After preparing a pile of this material, a sufficient amount of organic nitrogen (e.g., manure, dried blood, green grass clippings, *etc.*) must be added and mixed into the pile. (Inorganic nitrogen fertilizer will not work.) Compost starters, which contain microorganisms and nitrogen, should be unnecessary, though you can add a little soil from your garden if you like. The pile must be kept moist and turned every 2-3 days to provide oxygen for the bacteria. This method of composting causes the material being composted to heat to over 100 degrees. (This is the same chemical process that causes silos to catch on fire with spontaneous combustion!) Recipes for doing this are available on-line if you are feeling very ambitious.

Since the two week method requires assembling all the materials up front - a problem when you are using kitchen scraps and yard waste - plus a lot of careful attention to details, it is very rare to find anyone who has had any success. Instead, our contributors use the "1 year method," which is to simply pile the materials as you generate them in a secluded area and allow the bacteria and earthworms to convert the material into "planting mix".

Compost heaps

If you have room, all you have to do is make a big pile of leaves, yard waste and kitchen scraps somewhere screened from view on your property and dump new material on top of the pile as you go. If the pile is a big enough, it will generate enough heat to keep the decomposing process going through part of the winter. With the ever popular one-heap method, when you want to use some compost, you just dig it out from the bottom. The pile should be turned once in a while to aerate it, though even without that, it will eventually decompose. Practically speaking, turning the pile comes to an end during the winter, or there never would be a stable bottom from which to remove the completed compost! You can also start a second pile in the spring and get your compost out of last year's pile.

Outdoor compost bins

Compost bins are really intended for use in the 14 day method. Although the fancy kinds such as the tumblers provide an easy way to aerate the materials, most people do not use them the way they were intended but rather continuously add scraps and never end up with a finished product. Since these bins are protected from the rain, the material may not compost at all because it is too dry. If you don't have room for a compost heap or have aesthetic objections, a large plastic trash can with holes drilled in the side for air makes an inexpensive bin which you can move around your garden on a hand truck.

Whatever method you use, it is nice to have someplace near your kitchen to dump scraps. You might want to use a bin for temporary storage, when your kitchen scraps are at their most wet and unattractive stage. Then periodically transfer the contents onto your heap, where the rain and worms can get at them. If you have a strong constitution or favorable architecture you could also keep the pile under your deck and toss scraps in directly from the kitchen.

Kitchen compost bins
To keep slimy scraps from sticking to the inside of your miniature bin, you can line it with Biobags compostable bags, available on line.

Kitchen scraps
Use uncooked vegetable scraps and coffee grounds but no animal products other than egg shells. Eggshells will contribute needed calcium to your garden, but they do take a long time to break down. You can speed that process by grinding them up with water in your blender.

Garden waste
Weeds are incredibly tenacious. Their seeds are not necessarily broken down by the composting process, even if you use the fast method. If you don't want to take a chance, put your diseased plants, weed parts that can regrow, and invasive plants into an opaque plastic bag to go into the trash. Alternatively, you could limit the areas in your garden where you apply compost to those areas where you will apply an adequate cover of mulch to suppress the weeds.

Worm farms
Worm poop ("castings") is said to be the *crème de la crème* of quality compost. Many, many worms are required. Worm farms have to be kept indoors in the winter and thus add lots of fruit flies to your ecosystem.

How to plant flowers, shrubs and trees

The standard planting method is to dig a hole twice as wide as the pot and slightly deeper, and fill it back in with amended soil. A simple soil recipe is a mixture of one half soil, one quarter Super Fine mulch, and one quarter compost. Alternatively, you can till the entire flower bed before you plant anything by digging out the soil to about ten to twelve inches, amending it, and putting it back in. Using a mantis (which is like a small rototiller) can make this task easier. This is also your opportunity to put in vole cages. Thoroughly preparing your garden bed makes planting a pleasure down the road.

However, there is new thinking among native plant experts that can simplify your life greatly. Many gardeners are moving away from tilling as a way to prepare a bed, because it unearths a lot of weed seeds which then sprout. Plus, rich, amended soil mixtures are totally unnecessary for many plants. In fact, some plants may do better if you just plunk them into the ground with a handful of compost. Overworking the soil is like over-teasing your hair: breaking down the soil structure is not good for it. For herbaceous plants, you can just dig a hole big enough for the pot. For shrubs, dig it twice as wide so as to have room to spread out the roots, but you don't need to dig it any deeper than the pot.

Of course, if the topsoil has been completely stripped as part of the house construction process, the remaining bare clay may need some amending. Northern Virginia has a clay soil that comes from feldspar. It is adequate in mineral content but is poor in porosity. Adding compost greatly improves the porosity of our soil, which is important for drainage and to allow roots to penetrate.

For shrubs and trees, try to replicate the natural environment as much as possible. Trees drop their leaves in the fall, those leaves break down and add organic matter and nutrients to the soil, those nutrients are cycled back up into the trees in spring, and the cycle is pretty much self-sustaining and closed. If you can mimic this, your trees and shrubs will most likely be happy. With a starter compost mulch on top and leaf cycling, not much else has to be done to keep the plants growing, except to make sure the plant gets plenty of water the first year. When the compost mulch, or the hardwood mulch, completely decomposes away, you can replace it, but this certainly won't be every year.

Uncomposted brown leaves contain a lot of carbon and not much nitrogen. If they are mixed or tilled into the soil, they can cause nitrogen deficiency. However, when used as a mulch, this is not really a problem.

Natives vs. "aliens"
The benefit of native plants is that they are accustomed to the local climate and soils. As long as you keep your soil in decent shape, natives should be happy. Aliens, on the other hand, may not be accustomed to our weather and soil. They may require richer soil or more moisture than would be naturally provided. This is when you have to get into more intensive care, such as fertilizing, frequent compost applications, pH adjustments and frequent watering. On the other hand, some aliens are all too happy in our environment and grow wild (think English ivy or kudzu). Natives generally have that "just right" blend – they are easy to care for but they don't grow wild.

Watering
Here is an interesting innovation: follow the standard planting directions and put the plant in the hole, raising it to the correct level. But

then fill the hole with water and let it drain out before filling in around the plant with dirt and watering again. This will thoroughly soak the root ball and the surrounding soil.

Plant annuals the first year

When creating a new garden bed, don't put in perennials initially: plant annuals instead. Their roots will help lighten the soil and add organic material.

Planting bulbs

It is much easier to do this job with two people: one to make the hole, the other to pop in the bulbs.

Dig holes one day, plant another

If you are planting more than a couple of plants, it is more efficient and less exhausting to spread out the work. Mail order plants need to go into the ground immediately. To assure that, you can dig the holes after you order them and while you are waiting for them to arrive.

Watering tips

How much should you water?

It is not at all easy to figure out how often and how much to water. Overwatering can be as bad as under watering. For most plants, the goal is to water enough to evenly soak the surrounding soil and the deepest roots - not just the top - and then let it nearly dry out before watering again. Ideally, you should check the plant before you water, either by feeling four inches down with your finger or by using a moisture meter (if you can find one that works) and hold off on watering until it is needed. Whether analyzing the needs of every plant on your property is really practical when you have limited time is another question.

For trees, the rule of thumb for each watering is to supply one gallon for every inch of tree trunk diameter. If using a hose, figure out how long it takes to deliver a gallon by timing it with a bucket. To allow time for the water to soak in gradually without running off, you can use a gator bag, buckets with small holes in the bottom, or a soaker hose wrapped in a spiral around the base of the tree.

A common recommendation is to water new plants daily for the first few days, then weekly for the first year, except in weeks in which the ground is frozen or in which you have measured an inch of rainfall (use a rain gauge and keep track). This may not be enough, though, depending on the heat, and may be too much in cool weather. Small plants in the summer - especially annuals - may need watering every two to three days or even more. Larger plants and trees may need it every three to five days. Trees need at least two years to become established, so keep up the watering on them longer.

For plants that need good drainage, there is another consideration: if you dig a hole in clay, that hole may collect water like a bowl and drown the roots. Some sources actually recommend digging a hole as wide as a card table when planting trees and shrubs (a tip that is more helpful to owners of back hoes than to the rest of us).

Plan around watering

We all go mad with planting in the spring, and if we are "in the know," we go mad again in the fall. But then you have to water all these plants for the next year. Simplify your life by concentrating on one area of your garden at a time. That way, you will not have to spend your time dragging a hose to every corner of your property.

What makes a good hose?

Better quality hoses cost more but are a pleasure to work with. The cheap ones kink, and the fittings can be more easily damaged. Brass fittings are more durable. The wider the hose, the faster the water can be delivered. Look for ⅝ or ¾ inch rather than the standard ½ inch size. This is especially important if you need an extra-long hose, have low water pressure, or are running water up hill. A hose made of rubber or PVC, with multiple layers and reinforcing mesh, will hold up better and kink less. Store the hose in the shade, because sunlight will gradually break down the material. Drain the hose and bring it in for the winter.

Soaker hoses are a little tricky to use. They are difficult to straighten out and rearrange into the shape you want, and they are prone to kinking and cracking. But once installed, they are the ideal way to water. Look for a professional grade product or one with a long guarantee. Stretch it out on a hot surface such as a black driveway to straighten out the stubborn curves. Lay it in place in your garden, hold it down with staples every couple feet, and cover it with mulch to keep the sun from causing it to dry up and crack. Some people take them up in the winter to make it easier to plant in the spring. A deep watering with a soaker hose typically takes about four hours.

A sprinkler system can obviously save you a lot of time. Elevated sprinklers on a timer can also work well. The drawback of sprinklers is that they waste a lot of water, since unnecessary areas get sprinkled and much of the water evaporates in the air.

How can you save water?
A secondary goal when watering is to avoid wasting water. Not only do you have to pay for it, but the delivery of drinkable water to your property takes a lot of community resources. Over a third of the drinking water in the United States is used on our lawns and gardens. Soaker hoses and drip systems deliver the water right where you need it, though they have the disadvantage that they get in the way of digging and weeding.

Water barrels with a spigot at the bottom are easy to situate under a downspout. Your roofer can connect them if you are not handy. Unfortunately, a rain barrel is not an easy way to water your garden unless you have it hooked up to a soaker hose. But if you think of rain barrels less as a source of water for your garden and more as a way to divert runoff from our storm sewers and streams, then they might make more sense. Rain barrels also can provide a source of unchlorinated water for filling ponds. Unfortunately, they also make fine habitats for mosquito larvae, so keep them carefully covered.

Your home has other sources of "free water." For instance, you can put a bucket in your shower to catch the water while it is warming up. (One of our contributors recommends this.) Some homes are built to separate the sewage from gray water, which can be used on plants.

Other garden stuff

Want lots of color in your garden? Think about this: deer (and beetles, fungi and rabbits) don't eat ceramic pots! Whether your "hardscape" ideas are as simple as a birdbath or a garden bench or as elaborate as terracing or stone walls, the non-living components of your garden should be considered right from the start. Features such as flags, fountains and obelisks draw the eye and anchor the landscape. And functional additions such as vole cages and soaker hoses are much easier to install before plants are in the way.

Keep edging simple
Many products are sold to create a distinct border for your garden, such as stones, railroad ties and metal strips. Most of them get crooked with time and start to look ramshackle. In addition, your lawn mower will not reach all the way to the edge, forcing you to edge the grass. Both these problems can be avoided by the alternative of a simple trench filled with mulch. Use a square shovel for this purpose. It is a fair amount of work the first year but easy enough to maintain after that.

Make a mowing strip
To make it easier to mow next to a wall or raised bed, lay down a strip of flat stones or bricks on the ground along the edge. Weeds will still grow up between them, though, so some edging will be required.

Arbors and trellises
Be careful what you train up an arbor, trellis or fence. You will not be able to paint or reseal wooden ones if they are covered with perennials.

And some vines are so strong that they will quickly tear apart a wooden structure. Wisteria is a good example of that.

Save the frogs

Swimming pools are like plastic flowers: they look good but don't actually create habitat. In fact, frogs and other animals die by the score when they are sucked into the skimmer and drowned. Luckily, there is a cure for that. Order a cute little skimmer escape ramp from <u>Critterskimmer.com</u>. It actually works!

Saving money: free stuff, bargains and other tips

Plants can definitely get expensive. Here are some ways to stretch your dollars.

Buy One, Get Ten Free
Some plants can be propagated by taking a cutting and sticking it in the ground to root. Examples include *Aucuba japonica*, hydrangeas and forsythia. Wet the end with water, dip in Root Tone powder, and plant in a hole with prepared soil. Chrysanthemums can be propagated simply by pushing a cutting into a pot or straight into the ground. Since trimming chrysanthemums in April and June shapes them into a nice mound, you can get plenty of clippings for this purpose then. This works best with the simpler mums; the fancier ones may not be as hardy. Many other kinds of plants can be propagated from cuttings using slightly more elaborate techniques, which are easily found on the Web.

Many shrubs, such as rhododendrons, can be multiplied by the following method. Take a lower side branch and push it onto the ground, burying it under a couple inches of soil. Put a heavy rock on top to hold it down. Take a look a year later. If it has rooted, clip its "umbilical cord" to separate it from its parent. You can leave it there to develop for another year, or go ahead and move it right away.

Divide plants
Many perennials benefit from being divided every few years. Simply dig them up and chop the root ball in half: delicacy is not called for. Read up on the best time to do this. Hostas, for instance, should be divided in the fall.

Volunteer
Volunteers at public gardens get to take home extra plants.

Plant exchanges
Invite your friends or members of your organization to bring their labeled plants, seeds or tools to an exchange in late April or early May.

Buy plants from farmer's markets
These markets sell plants in the spring, sometimes for a bargain.

Buy plants on sale
Scrawny-looking perennials may grow just fine in your garden. The seasonal garden centers that set up in the corner of our shopping centers typically close up by mid-summer and often put their stock on sale. The plants may look a little dog-eared but are often capable of a strong comeback. Buying plants on sale is a good way experiment with things you might not ordinarily try.

Plant things that self-seed
Some annual flowers will come back year after year, if not in exactly the same spot where you planted them originally. Examples include cosmos and cleome (spider flowers). In fact, cleome may self-seed a little too much for some people's taste! Wild phlox (*Phlox divaricata*), brown-eyed Susan (*Rudbeckia triloba*), butterly weed (*Asclepias tuberosa*), and native columbine (*Aquilegia canadensis*) are examples of perennials that spread themselves around by seed. Wait until they poke up before mulching your beds in the spring, as mulch smothers them as easily as it does weeds.

Check out Freecycle

Freecycle is a great way to get free plants, tools, bird baths, and anything else you need. You join the on-line Freecycle group in your neighborhood. Members can either offer or request items and then just go pick them up. 100% free. www.freecycle.org

Take advantage of free tree seedlings

Arlington County and Fairfax ReLeaf give away tree seedlings for free.

Band together in a seed co-op

Since seed packets usually contain far more seeds than you need, get together with some friends to share the seeds.

Have fun dumpster diving

People often throw out their pots of chrysanthemums after they finish blooming. You can rescue them and put them into a sheltered place for the winter. If they make it, you will have a nice new plant the next year.

Do some Easter scavenging

Easter lilies, hyacinths, and other flowering bulbs that churches use for decoration are often thrown out afterwards. Plant them in your garden, and they may come up next year.

Buy seeds early on sale

Seed companies discount their seeds in January and February, so planning early can pay off. You can save even more if you buy in the fall, but those will be year-old seeds. Germination rates fall off in time, but one year usually does not make a big difference.

Create your own gifts

Pick up inexpensive vases or other glassware from yard sales and fill them with cut flowers from your garden as presents.

Build your own netting frames
Use stiff electrical conduit pipes as uprights and ½ inch flexible PVC to connect them to create hoops over which you can drape your netting or floating cloth.

Make your own netting pins
Use giant nails stuck through the lid of a jar or plastic tub.

Construct your own greenhouse
If you have an old swing set, you could cover it with 4 mil clear plastic and hang a heavy duty plastic curtain for a door.

Save on topsoil for raised beds
Dig the soil out of the path next to the bed.

Hire a day laborer
If you have big ambitions but limited muscles and funds, you could hire one or two people to help you do the heavy work for a day. The Centreville Labor Resource Center is open 6 am to noon, Mondays through Saturday (as of winter 2011-2012).

Refurbish your clippers
Tools can be taken apart and cleaned and sharpened.

Build your own rain barrel
Fairfax County offers classes to teach you how for a big savings.

Save Think big box stores
You can often get the same fertilizer or mulch for less at the big outlets.

Fix your leaking garden hose fittings
When the fitting starts to leak, it is extremely easy to cut off the end of the hose and put on a new fitting rather than replace the whole hose.

Free plant tags
Plastic spoons and knives marked with an indelible marker make satisfactory, if temporary, plant markers.

Camouflage compost bins
An old garbage can with the bottom cut out is a good size for composting.

Free storage
Baby food jars are just the right size for storing seeds and dried herbs.

Use your own leaves
You could rake up your leaves, put them in bags at the curb, and have the county collect them to give away for free to a company that grinds them up and puts them in bags to sell back to you as "compost," "leaf mold," "planting mix," etc. Or you could just make a big pile and save them for a year or two until they break down. One way to move them is to rake them onto a big drop cloth and drag them to where you want them.

"Borrow" some horse manure
Horse owners may be happy to unload their manure if you ask them. For example, the Caisson Platoon at Fort Meyer in Arlington leaves its manure out for the public to take. Just drive up to the Fort Meyer gate and ask. It is best to compost manure first so it does not scorch your plants.

Build a trailer
You can buy a basic flatbed utility trailer at Harbor Freight Tools at Potomac Mills for under $300, then lay down a floor and put up plywood sides. It is great for hauling plants and mulch.

Take advantage of free mulch
See the separate section on mulch.

Use bamboo

You should never plant bamboo - it is horribly invasive and almost impossible to contain - but if it is already established, you can try to make the best of a bad situation. If you have some bamboo growing into your yard, perhaps from a neighbor's property, it is a perfect material to use for plant supports. Lash the bamboo together with some twine and you have a green trellis that blends in nicely with the live plants. It looks nicer than metal, and when the season is over you can always pull it out, save it or toss, as there will be more next season.

Gardening with children

Just as we nourish and tend to gardens to make them flourish, adults can inspire an appreciation and maybe even a love of gardens and gardening among young people in a number of different ways.

- Invite children to help in the family garden – weeding, watering, picking flowers, harvesting vegetables.
- Instill in your children a sense of ownership by giving them each a garden bed or row. Plant fast growing vegetables such as beans, radishes, carrots or lettuce. Cherry tomatoes and the bush type of sweet peas are fun because children can pick them, and eat them raw off the vine.
- Pumpkins are great for kids because the vine wanders all over. Plant a hill of pumpkins, one for each child in your neighborhood.
- Potatoes put on a good show. You can wait for the eyes to start to develop on an ordinarily potato, cut them out, lay them in soil, then add hay or grass clippings to cover them. This way you can peek at the potatoes as they start to grow.
- Start fun seeds and bulbs inside the house in the winter – avocados, sweet potatoes, grapefruit, beans, paper whites.
- Think colorful. Corn in wild colors is amusing; you can buy varieties in blue, black, dark green and yellow. Cucumbers come in orange, pink and yellow.
- Visit local botanical gardens, nature parks and nurseries together. Taking children to public gardens (instead of museums) is a great activity since they can run around. The American Horticultural Society's River Farm has an alphabet garden.

- When traveling or walking in the neighborhood, identify plant, flower, wildflower and tree varieties – as well as mammals, birds, butterflies and insects that are vital parts of our gardens and forests.
- Discuss and follow-up on interesting facts children learn at school through their science units on plants, trees, insects, earthworms – even poison ivy (a topic in first grade in Fairfax County Public Schools).
- Enjoy and support Eco-friendly activities; shop at farmers' markets; look for open spaces in cities and suburbs; find roof-top plantings.
- Pick your own. There are numerous farms in Loudoun and Fauquier counties (as well as one in Prince William county) that are open for picking your own fruits, vegetables and even flowers, starting with strawberries in the spring and running all the way to apples and pumpkins in the fall. Some offer other entertainment as well for the kids. You can find them at www.pickyourown.org.
- Share books about gardens and related topics – nonfiction and picture books, even folk tales and poetry.
- Visit websites created to foster environmental literacy.

Books for children

Picture books

Mayer, Mercer Green, *Green Garden (I Can Read)* (Early elementary, for beginning readers)
> Little Critter learns that gardens are fun but lots of work.

Stevens, Janet, *Tops and Bottoms* (Early elementary)
> Clever Hare plants a vegetable garden and tricks lazy Bear into giving him the best produce.

Krauss, Ruth, *Carrot Seed (Board Book)* (Preschool)
> In this 1945 classic, a little boy is undaunted as he plants a seed and waits for it to grow.

Shannon, George, *Busy in the Garden* (Preschool-early elementary)
> Humorous poems and riddles make gardening sound like fun.

Legends and folktales

Lunge-Larsen, Lise, *Legend of the Lady Slipper (Ojibwe Tale)* (Elementary)
> Native American tale of a brave little girl who ventures out in a snowstorm for healing herbs, leading to the beginning of a new flower.

Peck, Jan, *The Giant Carrot* (Elementary)
> Russian tall tale of a family's teamwork that results in a gigantic veggie.

DePaola, Tomie, *Legend of the Bluebonnet: An Old Tale of Texas* (Elementary)
> Fifteen year old boy and younger sister cross the border from Mexico to join their parents in California in this realistic survival story.

Kellogg, Steven, *Jack and the Beanstalk*
> The illustrations in this version are particularly gorgeous and engaging.

Osborne, Mary Pope, *Kate and the Beanstalk*
> Strong female character has an adventure similar to Jack's in this lesser known folktale.

Powell, Patricia Hruby, *Blossom Tales: Flower Stories of Many Folk* (Elementary)
> Collection of short legends from around the world "explaining" the origin of 14 different flowers.

Tolstoy, Aleksei, *The Gigantic Turnip.*
> Many versions exist of this old story of a farmer whose turnip grows so huge he needs lots of help pulling it out.

Nonfiction books

Burnie, David, *Bug Hunter: Nature Activities* (Elementary)
> Activities to promote understanding, observation and fun, firsthand experience with insects, earthworms.

Smucker, Anna Egan, *Golden Delicious: A Cinderella Apple Story* (Elementary)
> True account in picture book format of discovery of a new variety of apple - the golden delicious.

Mikula, Rick, *Family Butterfly Book: Discover the Joy of Attracting, Raising & Nurturing Butterflies* (Upper elementary – adult)
> Background information on butterfly species, how to make a butterfly garden, raising caterpillars.

Ready Set Grow! Quick and Easy Gardening Projects (Elementary)
> Numerous child-friendly projects from garden basics to crafts, containers and indoor sprouting.

Richardson, Beth, *Gardening with Children* (Families)
> Practical tips and steps for parents who want to share the joy and work of gardening with children.

tomato

More advanced tips

Check the drainage
Any land on a slope will automatically be well drained, whatever the soil texture. By contrast, for plants that ordinarily need it to be a little marshy, a base of clay on a flat surface may catch enough water to allow them to survive.

Deadhead or not?
Perennials mostly bloom only once in a year. However, if you shear some plants after they flower, they may flower again. Do an Internet search on "Garden Gate Magazine Deadheading" to find a nice list. However, many plants will reseed if you let them, and the seeds of some - such as purple coneflower - will feed the birds, so don't be in too much of a hurry to cut things back.

Fall cleaning or not?
Many gardeners like to clean out their flower gardens in the fall, mostly for the manicured look. They may also have a theory that tender plants might have trouble pushing up through matted leaves in the spring, and that little varmints might nest in the litter. However, a fall cleaning is definitely not a requirement, except for diseased plants. Leaving the other leaves and stems in place benefits the insects that live on them and is good for the soil. After all, this is what happens in the wild. In the spring, you can simply cut back the dead stems to tidy it up before things start growing.

Shear some plants in May to make them grow fuller
Certain plants tend to get leggy and flop over when they flower. After they have grown enough, you can cut them back by a third or a half and end up with much fuller, shorter plants. Examples include tall sedum, chrysanthemums, cat mint and balloon flowers.

Make your own plant nursery
To multiply your plants, find a place with conditions that are as gentle as possible: not too much wind or sun, but exposed to the rain. Underneath a deck or a tallish tree may work. Here you can propagate your plants without going to very much trouble. For instance, you can take little volunteers that have grown up, plant them in plastic pots, and see if they make it through the winter. Tree seedlings, forsythia, chrysanthemums - and other plants that have sprung up in random locations - are all good candidates for this approach. Some will flourish, some won't, but your investment is negligible and you will end up with quite a few strong plants that you can use yourself or give away. Your home nursery is also a good place to quarantine plants that have been given to you by friends, since you can keep them there until you see that they are weed free.

Sterilize your pruners
When you shear or prune plants like holly or peony with scale or mildew, spray the pruners with alcohol to prevent the infestation from spreading to other plants you may be pruning.

Scrub out pots
Dirty pots, particularly those left over from dead plants, may harbor diseases. Wash them out thoroughly. You may want to soak your re-used clay pots in a solution of household bleach.

Curb that garden
The strip of ground between the sidewalk and the street is a perfect place for a garden which will really be appreciated by your neighbors. Petunias to spill over the curb, small roses and other shrubs, and "step-

pable" ground cover or liriope to fill in the spaces in between make a lovely combination.

Study in blue
Consider creating a garden with a color scheme, such as blue flowers and silvery foliage from lavender, lamb's ears and sea holly.

Some shrubs need mates
Certain shrubs are dioecious, meaning that they have male and female versions. The females produce the berries, but only if they are cross fertilized with a male, which should be planted fairly close by so the bees can fly back and forth. Examples include many hollies *(Ilex species)*, skimmias, aucubas, and yews. Other shrubs do not come in male/female but still cannot pollinate themselves. You have to plant at least two shrubs for either to produce berries. Examples include blueberries and some viburnums.

Grow food, not lawns
Blueberries and raspberries are easy to grow in this area, and they produce lots of fruit that you can eat or just let the birds enjoy. (You will need bird netting or bird tape if you want to be the one doing the eating).

Nature abhors a vacuum
Bare, open ground, especially disturbed soil that gets some sun, is a magnet for invasive weeds. Plan to substitute something else, or mulch, before the weeds move in.

Don't let your bird feeder kill your plants
Sunflower seed husks contain substances that inhibit plant growth. When chemicals from one plant are toxic to another, that phenomenon is called allelopathy. (Another example of allelopathy is the black walnut tree *(Juglans nigra)*. The uncomposted leaves, nuts and every other part of the tree are toxic to many plants, so it is hard to grow things underneath.) You can solve the bird feeder problem by buying husk-less bird food.

Why "The holly and the ivy?"
If you have an American (or English) holly tree, you may have found out why, "Of all the trees that are in the wood, the holly bears the crown." That is because its branches reach all the way down to the ground and form a handy ladder for vines to grow on. If you don't like that effect, one option is to remove the lower limbs.

Soil testing

You hear a lot about soil testing, but home gardeners seldom bother with it. However, if you have some plants that are not growing as well as they should, or if you are starting a new garden, it could be useful to find out if your soil has unexpected deficiencies. And certain plants, such as blueberries, simply cannot be grown without the proper pH.

The soil around here is mostly acidic. Our predominant native forest is oak, which likes acid, and which sheds acidic leaves. In fact, the whole east coast has acidic soil naturally, because the rocks themselves are acidic and the moisture conditions are right to keep the soil that way. You will mostly be fighting a losing battle if you try to grow alkaline loving plants; this is one of the problems with turf grass, since lawns require lime to raise the pH to the 6.5-7 range. Conversely, you will usually be happy with acid loving plants such as rhododendrons (so long as you can find the sheltered environment they require).

There are exceptions to our acidic soil. For example, lime may leach from the foundation of your house, making the nearby soil alkaline. Therefore a rhododendron may not be a good foundation plant. And, of course, if you spread lime on your property, the pH will rise. Acid loving plants will get pretty sickly in alkaline soil. To find out what you really have, you can mail or bring in a soil sample to the Virginia Cooperative Extension, which has offices in Fairfax, Arlington, Manassas and Leesburg. Soil testing mailers are available at public libraries and at the Master Gardener booths at farmers markets. The lab will send you an extensive analysis of the mineral content of your soil and its pH, with recommendations for what you need to add to the soil in order to grow specific plants. You can also test the pH yourself with a home kit

Daffodil

Why go native?

Short Answer

Plants that come from our area are adapted to live here, in our acidic clay soil, hot weather, and long periods of drought, with a minimum of human assistance. Using them in our gardens frees us from having to water as much and from using pesticides or other chemicals to keep them alive. But more importantly, unless suburbanites start growing native plants in their gardens, more and more birds and frogs will die, and fewer and fewer species of plants and animals will survive in the United States.

Much longer answer

In his fascinating (if alarming) book *Bringing Nature Home*, Douglas Tallamy lays out in very readable terms the science behind the trend toward natives. If you read his book, you will never want to buy an alien ornamental again.

The biggest reason for loss of species (plant or animal) is loss of habitat. The lower forty-eight is down to under five percent of undisturbed land. The rest is suburban, urban or farmland. The remaining five percent is increasingly broken up into pieces that are too small to sustain many species. It is predicted that in time, we will lose a proportionate number of plant and animal species (in other words, over ninety-five percent) from simple loss of habitat.

Insects are a crucial part of the food chain, themselves providing the food for most higher species of animals. Without enough insects, most birds, reptiles and amphibians, as well as their predators, will not survive. For a given insect, "habitat" may mean a single species of bush or tree. Your yard can provide the habitat needed for survival.

Native plants are what insects eat. Only a tiny fraction can survive on plants that are imported from other continents. For example, there are over four hundred native bee species in our region, many of which are dependent on specific native plants for survival. Planting alien ornamentals and turf grass is like planting plastic flowers: from a habitat point of view, your garden and lawn are a sterile desert.

Plants not only feed insects but also directly feed many birds. Nonnative honeysuckle, for example, displaces the native honeysuckle with its nutritious berries and instead provides a berry that is excessively high in sugar. Native vines that climb trees provide food for birds and shelter for bats. They also serve as the hosts for bugs that protect native trees.

The habitat that is left after we finish paving, building or plowing is under constant threat of infestation by invasive alien plants. Since most American insects cannot eat foreign plants, specimens that were imported for our gardens have no natural enemies and sometimes multiply out of control, crowding out or smothering American plants in the process. It is extremely difficult to predict which ornamentals will become invasive. Huge, huge swathes of land have been taken over by these plagues.

Importing plants also brings alien diseases which have already wiped out huge parts of our ecosystem. For example, the American chestnut used to be the dominant tree in our forests; it is now almost extinct. Imported diseases also wipe out crops, such as a bacterium that is threatening the Florida citrus industry.

If a plant is poorly adapted to our climate, we can only keep it alive by seriously altering its environment. Turf grass, for instance, is almost all alien and requires huge amounts of water plus fertilizer, herbicides and lime (not to mention the gas in our polluting lawn mowers). And obviously, if you use pesticides, you will be directly eliminating the entire insect world wherever you put it. Most fescues are alien, as is Kentucky bluegrass (despite the name), ryegrass and zoysia. Tall fescue is actually invasive in Virginia.

The bottom line: if we value butterflies, frogs and birds, we must provide them with the food they need to live and reproduce. We must provide them with native plants. And the only place we have left to do it, after we use the rest of our land for pavement, buildings and cropland, is in our gardens.

On an immediate, practical level, native plants can make your life a lot easier. If you put the right plant in the right spot, once it is established the first year, it should not need watering afterwards. Fertilizer is unnecessary and possibly even counterproductive, depending on the plant. Leave the seed heads in place for the birds to feed on and resist the temptation to cut everything back for the winter.

What Counts as Native?

To produce usable habitat, you need not be a purest and confine yourself to plants that are native to the Potomac Valley. Very roughly speaking, plants that are native to any of the Mid-Atlantic states or in many cases even just the east coast will attract local insects that can thrive on them. And cultivars of those natives will have most of the same qualities, although there are exceptions. (When humans select for unusual varieties, it is often because of the unusual flowers. Small changes in the shape of a flower may make it impossible for insects to reach inside them to eat.) A hybrid, in which one species is crossed with another, is harder to evaluate, since if a native is crossed with an alien, you will have no way of predicting how it will perform as habitat. If two natives are crossed, you are probably safer.

79

Of course, just because a plant is native to this part of the country does not mean it will necessarily perform well in your garden. A swamp shade species may not think much of your sunny, dry window box!

The term "naturalized" is sometimes used to refer to a plant that invaded so long ago that it almost seems like a native. Queen Anne's lace *(Daucus carota)* is a common example. But even species that have lived here since the first Europeans arrived are still plastic plants as far as our insects are concerned. Evolution takes millennia, not centuries.

Native ≠ boring

Natives can by showy, too. You need not give up bright colors to go native. For example, if you have a sunny, dry location, you could create a spectacular garden with a background of shrubs such as arrowwood viburnum (*Viburnum dentatum*) and small trees such as serviceberry (*Amelanchier canadensis*). There are many good choices for yellow flowers, including seaside goldenrod *(Solidago sempervirans)* and black-eyed Susan (*Rudbeckia hirta*). For purple, wild bergamot (*Monarda fistulosa*) and New York ironweed (*Vernonia noveboracensis*) stand out. Add clumps of switchgrass (*Panicum virgatum*) for texture.

Fitting into the ecosystem

We can help restore habitat in our own back yards, one plant at a time. Here are some ways to do it.

Take the "Healthy Garden Pledge"
Create healthy habitats in your yards by planting native species, removing invasive plants, reducing pesticide use, conserving water, protecting water quality, and keeping birds safe.
www.audubonathome.org/pledge

Or...the "Plant More Plants" pledge
See www.plantmoreplants.com, the Chesapeake watershed site. Cute videos.

Make your property a wildlife sanctuary
Your garden can help save species from extinction. See details on the Audubon at Home web page. The fact sheets go into detail about what kind of plants to use to attract various species of birds, butterflies and other creatures. If you decide to go the whole way, you get a cool lawn sign to display!

Pull out invasive plants
And don't plant more!

Keep your water on your property
Prevent run-off by capturing all the rain that falls on your property. See the section on rain gardens for details.

Hire a responsible lawn care service
If you need a lawn and need someone to take care of your lawn, you can consult the Virginia Department of Conservation and Recreation list of lawn care operators that have agreed to Bay-friendly practices. www.dcr.virginia.gov/stormwater_management/documents/wqagree.pdf

Leave the tree trunks
Birds and other creatures need dead trees for shelter. When cutting down a tree, if possible leave some of the trunk standing. A stump of twenty feet is short enough to not do much damage if it falls over, and even twelve feet is high enough to provide useful shelter.

Create brush shelters
You can create more places for animals to hide and nest by using materials you have lying around. Start with a base of logs or possibly even PVC pipe or concrete blocks, and then pile brush on top. The idea is to create hidey-holes with entrances at ground level. Six feet tall is recommended, but smaller piles may also be useful.

Put up bird houses
Tree swallows and bluebirds could use our help in this regard.

Keep the cats indoors
House cats wreak havoc on the songbird population, killing hundreds of millions.

The world is your garden

You can think of your yard as your contribution to beauty, health and happiness. Or you can think even bigger and consider the entire region to be your scope. Here are some suggestions about how you can make the whole world your garden.

Volunteer at a public garden
All the public gardens need help. Just ask.

Become a master gardener
Master gardeners have completed a course offered by the Virginia Extension Cooperative and use their skills as volunteers at park clinics, demonstration gardens, and other educational venues. http://mgnv.org/

Join a garden club
Band together with other gardeners to learn about gardening and do gardening projects. Every club is different. To find one near you, call the National Capital Area Garden Clubs, Inc. at 202-399-5958 or go to www.ncagardenclubs.org.

Join a garden society
See the Resource section for information about a variety of societies, most of which have educational events, shows and newsletters. Examples include societies for lovers of camellias, roses, Green Springs Garden, mums, lilies, etc.

Join the American Horticultural Society
Membership gets you the monthly American Gardener magazine and free entrance to 65 gardens across the country.

Plant trees
Fairfax ReLeaf helps restore native trees on public land. www.fairfaxreleaf.org

Be a Tree Steward
TreeStewards are volunteers dedicated to improving the health of our urban trees through educational programs, tree planting and care, demonstrations and tree maintenance throughout the community. There are TreeSteward chapters in Fairfax and Arlington/Alexandria. www.treesvirginia.org.

Give the gift of trees with ReForest Fairfax
For a $35 donation, five native trees will be planted in Fairfax County in honor of your gift recipient. To order, visit the Restoration Project's website. www.fcrpp3.org

Get to know your District Urban Forester
Each Fairfax County district is represented by an Urban Forester. This is the person to call if you see misuse of open space or unauthorized tree cutting,

Help rid our region of infestations of invasive plants
See the chapter on invasives for details.

Restore habitat, garden at group homes, help clean streams, and more
Volunteer Fairfax offers numerous opportunities to join others on a wide variety of projects. www.volunteerfairfax.org. Other jurisdictions have similar on-line clearing houses for volunteers.

Join Project BudBurst on line
The mission of Project BudBurst is "to engage people from all walks of life in ecological research by asking them to share their observa-

tions of changes in plants through the seasons." All you have to do is observe one plant and put your results on line. Volunteering could not be easier! http://neoninc.org/budburst/index.php

Be a Wildlife Mapper
Help perform field studies that contribute to the state's biological databases. www.dgif.virginia.gov/wildlifemapping

Join a stream monitoring team
Teams of volunteers across the region meet once a quarter for two or three hours to monitor the health of our streams. It is a lovely, relaxing way to enjoy nature. Google "stream monitoring" and your county's name to find these programs.

Help monitor wildlife
Join other volunteers to monitor our populations of butterflies, birds, dragonflies, and other wildlife. http://www.audubonva.org

Become a master naturalist
Master naturalists are "volunteer educators, citizen scientists, and stewards helping Virginia conserve and manage natural resources and public lands." A total of 48 hours of training and 40 hours of volunteer work are required. The training program is offered through chapters in Arlington, Fairfax, Prince William and Loudoun.
www.virginiamasternaturalist.org

Recruit your neighbors
Start an environmental group in your neighborhood. Organize an environmental educational night. Speakers from the National Wildlife Federation (which has headquarters in Arlington) and the Audubon Society often will talk to a neighborhood group free of charge.

Feed the hungry
Too much zucchini? Donate your fresh produce to a local food bank

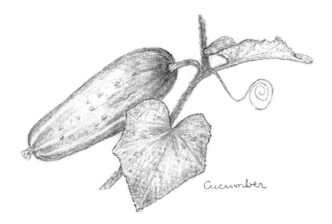

Cucumber

How to deer-proof your garden

Okay, the deer were here first. But the first time they take out 90% of your new plantings, you will start thinking of them as giant vermin. Ever wonder why your azalea only has two flowers blooming at the very bottom of the bush? The deer gave the plant a nice pruning.

There are several basic strategies for gardening in Bambi land.

Repellents
You can find dozens of smelly products for this purpose including garlic sticks, dog or human hair, dried blood (comes in pre-filled stakes), smelly bars of soap (Irish Spring bars strung every 3 feet on a string tied to stakes and surrounding the garden), sprays made of Godzilla urine, *etc*. Men may get a kick out of using their own urine; dog owners may want to brush their dogs outdoors and leave their hair in the garden. These methods may lull you for a while, but you are taking a big chance if you rely on them. One missed application or heavy rainfall, and your garden is deer candy. Even with assiduous work on your part, the deer may eventually decide to just hold their noses and eat anyway. Periodically switching from one method to another seems to be more successful than relying on one kind alone.

Fear
Solar powered blinking red lights are available which you mount four on a post and move around from time to time. The deer (or other raiding animals) apparently think it is the eyes of a predator and are scared away. Motion-triggered water sprayers also work well for some.

Keep out of reach

Containers on a high deck may be the best place for some of your plants. Hostas make fabulous container plants for a shady deck. Vegetables can be grown in containers in sunny spots. Back at ground level, if you plant your tempting items behind others that the deer hate, they might stay away. For instance, you could plant your lettuce inside a square of garlic plants.

Wire fencing cages

Building a cage around your garden beds might be a reasonable solution for vegetables.

Exclusion fences

If there is any way you can fence off your property, you will be in gardener's heaven. This is the best investment you can ever make. Buy rolls of heavy-duty 10 foot wide black plastic netting made for this purpose and attach it to trees and tall stakes, with gates where needed. In the woods, it is virtually invisible; even out in the open, it is not overly obtrusive. Ten feet is none too tall for a deer fence, but slightly shorter ones will usually do. You might even get away with a six foot fence, since deer are creatures of habit and may only need to be discouraged; however, with a fence that short, you will occasionally need to let a deer out, with luck before he or she eats the whole garden. Deer fencing comes in different grades: heavy, light and medium. A running deer will bounce right off the strong stuff. Electric fences might work even if they are short enough to jump over. You are just trying to get the deer to change their routines, and a shock to the shin may do it.

Plant what they hate

They say if a deer is hungry enough, it will eat anything. Certainly it will eat many of the items that are found on lists of deer resistant plants. There are a few plants, though, which our contributors have found to stand the test, and others which may be occasionally browsed but not seriously damaged. As a woman at a local nursery once said, deer could eat ornamental grass, but why should they? There is plenty of other grass for them to eat! And deer avoid certain other plants because they are toxic, too fuzzy, or smell like perfume. Thorns are no deterrent, though. See our perennial and annual lists for suggestions. Rutgers University has a nice searchable web site to look up plants. Find it by Googling "Rutgers Deer Resistant Plants."

Dogwood

How to vole-proof your garden

Voles are little rodents that tunnel underground. If you ever run water from the hose into one of their holes to see where the water will emerge, you will be amazed to see that it never does: the tunnel systems are huge. Should you be digging a planting hole and come across a vole tunnel, do not think of it as a convenient work saver to make your digging easier. If you plant there, your efforts are doomed. Voles snip off plants at ground level and gnaw away at shrubs and trees.

Not every garden has voles. They don't tunnel through gravel, for instance. But if you do have them, you need to take precautions up front.

By far your best bet is to install vole cages in your garden. The term is a little misleading, since it is actually your plants, not the voles, that get caged. This takes a really large amount of work, but it is well worth it! Buy a roll of wire fence cloth (this is like chicken wire with smaller holes) and cut it into lengths. Bend the sides and ends up to make a trough. Dig a big hole in your garden, put in the cage so the edges are just higher than ground level, fill with soil, and then plant inside the cage's perimeters. Heather Hill Gardens can show you their examples: all their hostas are protected by vole cages.

The best time to install a vole cage, of course, is when you first create a raised garden. The troughs can be as long as the garden.

Alternatively, sprinkling mole repellent may be temporarily effective.

You also can try filling the holes with the type of gravel that is usually sold as a soil lightener. Voles do not like to dig through gravel.

Some methods that do not seem to work include poison peanuts and vibrating objects that you insert in the ground (operated either by electricity or by a little windmill).

Columbine

Other critters

For groundhogs and bunnies, use two foot tall wire fencing. To really do a proper job, buy wider material and bury it all around to prevent burrowing.

Raccoons go wild over corn, so planting it will really attract them to your garden. If you can do without corn, you will have less of an issue. In fact, cornbread is just the bait for trapping raccoons, which you can do with a Have-A-Heart trap. If you release the raccoon within a few miles of your house, though, it is likely to find its way home again.

For people who know enough about handling electricity, installing electric fences may cut down on the raccoon damage, though probably not eliminate it. One electric fence technique that can keep out raccoons, and also rabbits and groundhogs, is to run two electrified wires around the garden, one at 4 inches from the ground and the next at 8 inches. String a third wire that is not electrified at 12 inches to keep birds from landing and being electrocuted. It is also important to keep vegetation trimmed away from the wires to discourage birds as well as to prevent short circuits. Run a fourth wire about 3-4 feet off the ground. On this top wire, string cut up pieces of Irish Spring soap along it at 3-4 feet intervals. Electric fences require a grounding wire which will not work if the ground is too dry: you actually have to water the soil around the wire in dry weather.

Alternatively, you can electrify an existing fence by running live wires at 4 and 16 inches (held away from the fence with insulators) and a grounding wire in between. None of this should be attempted by the inexperienced.

Since you can't tell if your electric fence is live just by looking at it, buy a volt meter. Testing the wire with your hand might just train *you* to avoid your garden!

Japanese beetles

If you don't like Japanese beetles, your best bet is to avoid planting beetle food. Traditional roses, hardy hibiscus, and hollyhocks end up being stripped bare by Japanese beetles. Knock Out roses, by contrast, are totally free of this problem.

Don't use insecticides
Insecticides kill everything in sight and are not so great for the birds and other animals that eat them, either.

Don't buy Japanese beetle traps
These traps attract the beetles with pheromones, which are essentially love potions for bugs. You end up attracting all the beetles in your neighborhood to your house, creating a dreadful scene of carnage without reducing the numbers that are eating your plants.

Make your own beetle juice
For an even more thoroughly repellent experience, one of our contributors grinds up some Japanese beetles in an old blender, mixes with water, strains it, and sprays the liquid on his plants. Apparently the survivors flee in horror.

Use milky spore
The general consensus is that the most effective and environmentally friendly way to reduce the infestation is to sow your property with milky spore, which kills the larval form of the Japanese beetle. *Paenibacillus popillia* (milky spore) is a bacterium that is sold in a powdered form. It is

the perfect biologic weapon, because it only kills Japanese beetles and supposedly nothing else. You put a little bit on your lawn every few feet, and over the course of a few years, the population of grubs (the larval form) is significantly reduced. It is a slow process, and - if you have a small yard - you might want to talk your neighbors into joining you, so you don't have their adult Japanese beetles flying into your yard.

Why remove invasive aliens?

Those of you in a hurry to establish a garden may be thinking: invasive beats brown! If so, resist the temptation.

Kudzu was introduced to the United States deliberately to prevent soil erosion. Who knew? So, however great you think it would be to have a single specimen of one of the plants on the "Do Not Plant" list in your garden, think about how our region will look if that species takes over. The Bradford pear is an easy example to appreciate. Yes, those miles and miles of white flowering trees in the spring are a gorgeous sight, but where they are, natives cannot grow. See chapter on "Why go native" to learn why losing natives is a very bad thing.

Other vivid examples of infestation of invasive aliens can be seen by the side of the road as you drive around the Beltway or down many of the other roads in our area. As you look a little more closely at what you thought was nice lush green, you realize that really what you are seeing is more like a horror movie: alien honeysuckle, oriental bittersweet, wisteria and other vines are completely taking over large swaths, climbing over trees and shrubs, and annihilating them. Once you are aware of this, you will be itching to leap out of your car and start yanking!

There are thousands of species of plants in the United States that originated elsewhere and are now thoroughly established here. The Virginia Native Plant Society, the Virginia Department of Conservation and Recreation and others have compiled lists of these plants that seriously threaten the environment in Virginia. Over ninety are nevertheless still available for sale, either in our local nurseries or from catalogs. See our list and please -- do not buy them!

Of the plants on the list that are important to avoid, a third are so terrible that you should actually kill them off if you already have them growing on your property. Many would be no great loss to you, but a few need special notes. You may have a lot of qualms about chopping down your Bradford pear or your butterfly bush, but please consider doing so. The Bradford pear may look beautiful while it is in bloom, but it is easily damaged by storms and is not really a satisfactory part of your landscape design. And the butterfly bush may attract adult butterflies to feed, but it does not actually contribute to the health of the butterfly population because its leaves do not support the caterpillars.

It's a little harder to know what to do about the other two thirds of the plants on the list. Certainly you should not buy them, but should you remove plants that you already have? Japanese pachysandra for instance, invades by way of its spreading runners, so if your patch is thoroughly isolated from the woods, you might be able to contain it. However, if there is no natural barrier such as a driveway, it will spread inexorably. Controlling this spread once begun would require a huge amount of work on your part, and when you sell the house, it is unlikely that your successors will keep up the defense. If you cannot bring yourself to remove these plants, at least edge your lawns to keep the turf grass out of the woods, and do your best to keep any other invasive plants you have from spreading.

Your neighbors may offer you some of their plants that grow in abundance. Beware: invasive plants are tough and easy to grow and thus likely to be donated to plant exchanges!

Vines, often used as ground-covers, are particularly problematic. By their nature, they are aggressive at least to a certain extent, since to be a successful ground-cover, they need to spread and form a nice mat. English ivy escapes into the woods, climbing up trees and slowly killing them. Goutweed, so lovely and tempting with its variegated leaves, is on the bad invasive list. All the white flowering honeysuckles are alien invaders (the native alternative has red flowers).

Do not let any non-native vine grow up your trees or shrubs. Many form berries once they get up high which are eaten by birds and thus distributed throughout our woodlands. The twisting vines can strangle the trunks of trees, and their leaves block sun from the leaves of the tree. And the heavy load of vine and leaves at the top can actually bring down trees during a storm. It is okay to let native grapevines and Virginia creepers climb up trees (you probably do not want them smothering your shrubs, though) because our trees evolved with those vines and are accustomed to their load. Native vines provide shelter for bats and are the hosts for bugs that protect native trees.

One invasive alien that is no longer for sale may still be all over your garden: the multiflora rose. This is a scourge of our woods; please remove it wherever you find it. If it is too large to pull up, repeated cutting at the base will eventually kill it off.

Excellent native alternatives are available for all your favorite plants. The eastern redbud (*Cercis canadensis*) blooms at about the same time as the Bradford pear. The Audubon Society has a whole long pamphlet on alternatives to English ivy and Japanese pachysandra, including native pachysandra (*Pachysandra procumbens*) which spreads more slowly but is just as nice. See the resource list chapter for web sites with descriptions of good native alternatives.

Just because a plant is not listed as a problem in Virginia does not mean it is a good idea to buy it. For example, *Lamiastrum galeobdolon* is on the noxious weed list in other states, and it is easy to see that Virginia will not be far behind. Unfortunately, this lovely vine makes a great shade ground-cover specifically because it is so invasive. Other alien ornamentals have seemed innocuous enough when first imported and behaved themselves politely for decades before suddenly escaping and becoming a major ecological threat. Scientists have found it difficult to predict which plants have invasive potential, so the only safe thing to do is avoid aliens as much as possible.

Some plants are not on the official Virginia invasive species lists (yet...) but are still invasive enough to become a nuisance in your garden. Examples include purpletop vervain (*Verbena bonariensis*), lily-of-the-valley (*Convallaria majalis,* okay if you plant them in a well contained area), and Queen Anne's lace (*Daucus carota,* whose roots are nearly impossible to eradicate). There are even some native plants which you buy at your peril, such as trumpet creeper (*Campsis radicans),* obedient plant (*Physostegia virginiana*), and certain varieties of goldenrod *(Solidago).*

How to eliminate the aliens

When pulling out enemy aliens, you obviously do not want to throw any fruiting parts into your compost bin. Put them in a black bag in the regular trash and not in with the yard waste. If you are unable to uproot the plant, cut it off as low to the ground as possible. You can then either paint the stump with concentrated glyphosate (the ingredient in RoundUp) or triclopyr (Weed B Gon) or else wait for the plant to sprout again and then spray the leaves with the regular RoundUp or Weed B Gon.

Japanese stilt grass

Japanese stilt grass goes to seed in early September. You can prevent that by mowing it very short in late August. The seeds are viable in the ground for seven years. It also spreads by runners, so you can contain it by pulling it up at the edge of the lawn. You can also kill it with pre-emergence crabgrass killer. Pendimethalin, the active ingredient of Scotts Halts Crabgrass Preventer, is very toxic to aquatic animals, so it is important to keep it from running off into storm sewers, ponds and creeks. If it gets on your driveway or sidewalk, brush it off. All herbicides have the potential to kill certain desirable plants as well as having possible toxicity to animals and even humans.

English ivy
1. Pull it up as best you can; bag and discard. Alternatively, if you have a powerful lawn mower, mow it down.
2. Cover with 10 layers of newspapers.
3. Cover that with 2 inches of mulch.
Weed killer does not work well on English ivy because of its shiny cuticle. Pre-spraying with Dawn dish detergent may help.

Help rid our parks of alien invasives

Numerous opportunities (every Saturday, many Sundays and some weekdays) are available for volunteers to join teams working to pull up invasive plants from our public areas. Fairfax County Park Authority, the RiP (Remove Invasive Plants) in Arlington, the National Park Service Weed Warrior program, and Earth Sangha all have schedules on line. You do need training and permission to remove any plant on public land.

These are the plants that volunteers are trying to eradicate (depending on the park).

burning bush	Norway maple
multiflora rose	Japanese honeysuckle
Japanese barberry	bush honeysuckle
autumn olive	stiltgrass
privet	Asian wisteria
Bradford pear	Chinese lespedeza
Japanese pachysandra	tree of heaven
bamboo	garlic mustard
English ivy	porcelain berry
oriental bittersweet	mimosa/silktree
wineberry	mile-a-minute/devil's tear thumb

To quickly determine whether a plant is considered an undesirable invasive, look it up on the running list on www.invasive.org.

Oriental Bittersweet

Do Not Plant list

Scientific name	Common names	Remove	Comments	Type
Acer platanoides	Norway maple	yes	Kills the undergrowth. A real problem. Can completely take over a wooded area.	tree
Aegopodium podagrari	goutweed, herb gerard, bishop's weed, snow in the mountain, ground-elder	yes	If you let the smallest part of this lovely plant into your garden, it will totally take over and be impossible to eradicate.	ground-cover
Ailanthus altissima	tree-of-heaven, Chinese sumac, stinking sumac, varnish tree	yes	Damages sewers and structures, threatens agricultural and natural ecosystems.	tree
Ajuga reptans & cultivars	bugleweed, carpet bugle	yes	Jumps out of your garden into your lawn. Can be kept under control in gardens but should be removed near natural areas. Its purple flowers in the lawn may look pretty in the spring, but slowly it will replace your grass with its flat broad leaves.	perennial
Akebia quinata	fiveleaf akebia, chocolate vine	yes	Will overrun and smother other plants	vine
Albizia julibrissin	mimosa, silk tree			tree
Ampelopsis brevipedunculata	porcelain berry, amur peppervine	yes	A real problem. Remove.	vine
Artemisia vulgaris	mugwort			perennial
Arundo donax	giant cane			grass
Berberis thunbergii	Japanese barberry	yes	Large stands displace native species.	shrub
Buddleja davidii (Buddleia)	butterfly bush	yes	Not every variety is invasive, but if you don't know which you have, you should remove it. Virginia sweetspire is an excellent alternative that not only attracts butterfly adults but also feeds their caterpillars.	shrub
Callicarpa dichotoma & C. japonica	Asian beautyberry	yes	Replace with the American version.	shrub
Cardiospermum halicacabu	balloon vine, love in a puff			vine

Do Not Plant list

Scientific name	Common names	Remove	Comments	Type
Celastrus orbiculatus	oriental bittersweet	yes	Thick masses of vines sprawl over shrubs, trees and other plants, girdling them or shading them out.	vine
Cercis chinensis	Chinese redbud			shrub
Clematis dioscoreifolia (also known as C. maximowicziana, C. paniculata and C. terniflora)	Sweet Autumn clematis	yes	Keep clematis under control in garden by destroying new growth.	vine
Convallaria majalis	lily-of-the-valley			
Coronilla varia	crown-vetch			perennial
Cytisus scoparius	Scotch broom			shrub
Deutzia scabra	fuzzy deutzia			shrub
Egeria densa	Brazilian water-weed		Popular for aquariums, but multiplies and clogs waterways.	aquatic
Elaeagnus angustifolia	Russian or Oleaster olive	yes	All of these spread and form huge thickets. Should be removed and replaced with better behaved shrubs.	shrub
Elaeagnus pungeris	thorny elaeagnus			
Elaeagnus umbellata	autumn olive, Japanese silverberry, umbellate oleaster	yes		
Eragrostis curvula	weeping lovegrass			grass
Euonymus alatus	burning bush	yes	Threatens forests, coastal scrublands and prairies where it forms dense thickets; multiplies rapidly.	shrub
Euonymus europaeus	European spindletree			shrub
Euonymus fortunei	wintercreeper euonymus	yes	Crowds out native understory, smothers small shrubs and trees	vine and ground-cover
Fallopia japonica also known as Polygonum cuspidatum	knotweed, fleece flower	yes	Ruins stream banks.	perennial
Festuca elatior (F. pratensis)	tall fescue			grass

103

Do Not Plant list

Scientific name	Common names	Remove	Comments	Type
Firmiana simplex	Chinese parasol tree			tree
Galium odoratum	sweet woodruff, wild baby's breath			groundcover
Hedera helix	English ivy	yes	Forms an impenetrable mat, crowding out other species. Climbs up trees and eventually kills them. Do not put in your compost pile.	vine and groundcover
Hemerocallis fulva	orange daylily	yes	You can eradicate these by mowing them until they die out.	perennial
Hesperis matronalis	dame's rocket			biennial
Hibiscus syriacus	rose of Sharon	yes	Remove baby plants that sprout around it.	shrub
Imperata cylindrical	Japanese blood grass, blady grass, cogon grass, kunai grass	yes	Highly invasive, needs to be replaced.	grass
Ipomoea coccinea	red morning glory, redstar, Mexican morning glory			vine
Ipomoea purpurea	purple, tall or common morning glory		A big nuisance in your garden.	vine
Iris pseudacorus	yellow flag, yellow iris	yes	Invades wetlands and is impossible to eradicate. Highly invasive and should be eliminated. Easily replaced with Louisiana iris or other native.	perennial
Lagerstroemia	crepe myrtle		A developing threat.	shrub
Lespedeza bicolo	shrubby lespedeza			shrub
Ligustrum amurense	amur privet	yes	Privets form dense thickets that displace native species.	shrub
Ligustrum obtusifolium	border or blunt-leaved privet	yes		
Ligustrum ovalifolium	California privet	yes		
Ligustrum sinense	Chinese privet	yes		
Ligustrum vulgar	European or common privet	yes		

104

Scientific name	Common names	Remove	Comments	Type
Liriope spicata	creeping liriope		Use *liriope muscari* instead.	ground-cover
Lonicera fra-grantissima	sweet breath of spring			vine
Lonicera japonica	Japanese honeysuckle, including "Hall's honeysuckle" cultivar	yes	Extremely difficult to eradicate. It will strangle other plants by coiling around them. Leafs out earlier than most natives and forms dense thickets too shady for most natives. Dense growth impedes reforestation efforts.	vine
Lonicera maackii	Amur honeysuckle	yes		shrub
Lonicera morrowii	Morrow's honeysuckle	yes		shrub
Lonicera standishii	Standish's honeysuckle	yes		vine
Lonicera tatarica	Tartarian honeysuckle	yes		vine
Lotus corniculatus	birdsfoot trefoil			perennial
Lunaria annu	money plant		Alba variegata is okay but do not plant the type with pink flowers.	biennial
Lysimachia clethroides	gooseneck loosestrife			ground-cover
Lysimachia nummlaria	creeping Jenny, moneywort	yes	Aggressive. Remove.	ground-cover
Lythrum salicaria and Lythrum virgatum	purple loose-strife and European wand loose-strife	yes	Horrible threat to the environment. Crowds out cattails, which are needed by various birds.	perennial
Mahonia bealei	leatherleaf mahonia			shrub
Melia azedarach	Chinaberry			tree
Melilotus officinalis	yellow sweet clover			grass
Miscanthus sinensis	maiden grass, Chinese silvergrass		Cultivars are less invasive but this is highly flammable and should not be planted next to buildings or where there can be danger of fire.	grass
Morus alba	white mulberry			tree

105

Scientific name	Common names	Remove	Comments	Type
Myriophyllum aquaticum	parrot's feather		Clogs waterways. This is often sold as an aquarium plant or by pond suppliers. It's okay as long as it is kept in your pond and not where it can get into any other body of water. Never throw it in stream, rivers, or natural ponds.	aquatic
Nandina domestica	nandina			shrub
Oenothera speciosa	pink ladies, pink sundrop, pink evening primrose, Mexican primrose, showy evening primrose, amapola			ground-cover
Pachysandra terminalis	Japanese pachysandra, Japanese spurge			ground-cover
Paulownia tomentosa	princess, empress, foxglove tree	yes	Invades forests, stream banks and some rocky habitats.	tree
Pennisetum alopecuroides – black-flowered cultivars like 'Moudry'	black flowered fountain grass		Use the buff colored varieties of fountain grass.	grass
Perilla frutescens	beefsteak plant, perilla mint, Chinese basil, wild basil, purple mint, rattlesnake weed, summer coleus	yes	Pushes out native plants; poisons cattle.	annual
Phalaris arundinaceae	reed canary grass, ribbon grass	yes		grass
Phellodendron amurense	Amur corktree			tree
Phleum pratense	Timothy			grass
Phragmites australis	common reed	yes	Degrades wetlands wildlife habitat.	perennial

Do Not Plant list

Scientific name	Common names	Remove	Comments	Type
Phyllostachys species	bamboo	yes	Your neighbors will hate you forever as it invades their property, since nothing short of a nuclear weapon can eliminate it. To add insult to injury, it is highly flammable and therefore a fire hazard!	shrub
Polygonum cuspidatum Also known as *Fallopia japonica*	knotweed or fleece flower	yes		perennial
Populus alba	white poplar			tree
Pyrus calleryana	Callery pears (including Bradford pear)	yes	Crowds out other species. Spreads far and wide when birds eat the seeds.	tree
Quercus acutissim	sawtooth oak			tree
Ranunculus ficaria	lesser celandine	yes		perennial
Rhodotypos scandens	jetbead			shrub
Rosa wichura-iana	memorial rose			shrub
Salix alba and its hybrid S. × sepulcrali	white willow and weeping willow			tree
Securigera varia	crown vetch, purple crown vetch			ground-cover
Spirea japonica	Japanese spirea, mead-owsweet	yes	Spreads fast, shades out natives.	shrub
Ulmus pumila	Siberian elm			tree
Viburnum dilatatum	linden viburnum	yes	There are too many other good viburnums, native and non-native, to keep this one around.	shrub
Vinca minor and Vinca major	periwinkle, creeping myrtle	yes	Contain it in a garden by pulling it up where it sprouts.	ground-cover
Vitex agnus-castus	chaste tree			shrub
Vitex rotundifolia	beach vitex			shrub
Wisteria sinensi and floribunda	Chinese and Japanese wisteria	yes	Climbs up and kills trees by girdling them. Remove. There is an American alternative that is native.	vine

Fruits and vegetables

With our long growing season, Northern Virginia is well suited to growing produce, but you do need to know what you are doing. Raccoons and other critters would love to eat anything that the caterpillars and various blights leave behind. So even if you are casual about flowers, read up on the basics of vegetables and fruits before you start. With some planning, you can reap a bountiful harvest with little or no artificial chemicals.

When choosing what to plant, keep in mind that the weather can vary greatly from year to year. So, for example, it is a good idea to plant several varieties of peas. Some prefer a cool summer, some a hot summer, so among them you should have a harvest. Share the seed packages with a friend.

Don't plant vegetables too close together, or they will crowd each other out. Melons and squash are particularly problematic in this way: one vine can take over a huge part of your garden but deliver only a small yield, so don't plant them unless you have a lot of room.

Most people prefer to create a bed for vegetables separate from their flowers, but you can mix it up a little. If you plant flowers in the middle of your vegetable plot, it may attract pollinating bees. Marigolds may help deter slugs.

Planting a cover crop after you harvest is a way to add organic material to your garden, suppress weeds, break up compacted soil, and protect it from erosion. Some cover crops, such as hairy vetch, have the disadvantage that they survive the winter and are a big mess in the spring. More tidy are spring oats and forage (Daikon) radishes (*Raphanus sativus var. longipinnatus*). Winter freezes kills them, and then (in the case of spring oats) you rototill them under three to six weeks before spring planting time. (You do not want to incorporate fresh organic material into the soil right before planting, because the decomposition process will bind up nitrogen.) Forage radishes are even better than spring oats, because you do not need to till them under, and their deep tap roots are excellent for loosening the soil.

No room for vegetables? Rent a community garden plot. A total of 650 plots in nine Fairfax County parks are rented for $60-$65 per year, 200 in Arlington County at $50-$60, 70 in Leesburg for $45, *etc.* Waiting lists can be long, though.

What's easy to grow here?

Asparagus (with sandy soil), *celery, cucumbers, green beans, parsnips, peppers, pumpkins, raspberries, rhubarb* (also need sandy soil), *squash, tomatoes, yams* and *zucchini*. We have plenty of time to grow these with our long, hot summers.

Cool season crops can be tough to grow in the spring: it gets hot too fast here. But in the fall, our contributors have had success with *bok choy, broccoli, cabbage, carrots, kale, lettuce* and *spinach*.

What's harder to grow?

Artichokes need to be protected very carefully from the cold. One method is to bury them under six inches of mulch, which you remove in the spring. Damage from mold is a major problem.
Eggplants are a challenge. The flea beetles eat them right up.

Melons require a sandy soil to taste right and therefore do not do well in Northern Virginia.

Onions need special growing conditions (see below).

Strawberries are a lot of work because they need to be weeded a lot and because you have to bend over to pick them. They are a fun for kids, though (and for squirrels).

Which varieties should you buy?

There are a bewildering number of choices out there. Here are some of the ones recommended by our contributors.

Tomatoes

Some people strongly advocate heirloom tomatoes, finding them tastier and potentially less susceptible to bugs and disease, though lower in yield. Homestead and Rutgers are good choices.

Any of the commonly available hybrids should do well. Which one you pick will determine when you can expect to harvest. Early Girl, for instance, comes in earlier. You cannot reuse the seeds of hybrids, as they will not breed true.

Like some other plants, tomatoes can be divided into determinate varieties (bush tomatoes - more compact - which set all their fruit within a two week period then die) and indeterminate (vining tomatoes which grow and set fruit all season). Favorites in each category include:

> *Determinate* Roma (great for drying, among other things), Celebrity, Homestead, Rutgers, Mountain Pride (good choice for mid-late season)

Indeterminate Big Boy (these are in fact big), Juliet, Better Boy (good for canning), Early Girl (ready to harvest earlier), Fourth of July (harvest starts early, hence the name; bigger than cherry but smaller than regular tomatoes), and German Striped (red and yellow striped, delicious, though not acidic enough for canning)

Other crops

Asparagus - Jersey Giant. (Remember that sandy soil? The Garden State is made of sand). Jersey hybrids all come up the same size. The stalks of the Mary Washington variety come up different sizes but are more hardy and therefore a better choice for amateurs.
Beets - Red Ace
Corn - Gourmet Sweet White #378A (Stokes). This is a super sweet white hybrid. It does not need to cross pollinate, so you do not need to plant multiple rows.
Lettuce - Black-Seeded Simpson. New Red Fire (reddish leaves).
Green beans - Almost any cultivar will work.
Okra - Cajun Delight
Rhubarb - Valentine
Snap peas - RSVPea
Snow peas - Hoe Lan Dow
Spinach - Melody
Swiss chard - Neon Lights
Strawberries - The "alpine" variety is the best, producing very sweet, small berries from early spring to late fall. It has no runners.

Starting a new bed

By far the easiest way to grow produce is in a raised bed, which allows you to control the soil content and keep down weeds while saving your back. The walls should be twelve inches high, as some crops have deep roots, and the soil will not come all the way to the top. Start by laying down industrial weed block cloth, the kind with the 20 year guarantee. (The lighter, black kind of landscape cloth is not dense enough.) This prevents weeds from poking up from below. There are many kinds of materials available for the walls of a raised bed, such as wood (never use treated wood as the chemicals will leach into your food), composite plastics made from recycled material, galvanized steel, retaining wall brick, and stacked stone. You can even just pile some sticks if you don't mind a very casual look, or use an old tire for a cute miniature raised garden. The easiest method is to buy a snap together kit with the composite plastic boards, which are durable and reasonably attractive.

Fill your raised beds with a planting mixture such as equal parts peat moss, vermiculite and compost. For red raspberries, use a little less compost, as they need really good drainage. The premixed potting mixtures that contain fertilizer are generally not as good as a mix you control yourself.

Another traditional way to start a garden is to bring in a lot of organic material such as Leafgro and rototill it into the soil. You can kill the grass first by laying down 6 layers of newsprint and wetting it down. Do this about two months before tilling the soil.

Alternatively, no-till farming and gardening is becoming increasingly common, as it has been found to improve soil quality, reduce soil erosion, protect beneficial insects and soil microbes, and use less fuel. A simple method can be referred to as "lasagna gardening." Start with six inches of soil, manure and mulch. Keep adding to it every year. You will need to kill the grass first in this method as well.

Seeds *vs.* seedlings

Vegetable seedlings sold in garden centers do not always flourish after transplant. You do not know how the seedlings were treated. It usually works better to use really good quality seeds because your plants will have more vigor. Sowing directly in the ground saves work. Check the Virginia Cooperative Extension planting guides for the timing. Be sure to buy fresh seeds by consulting the date stamp on the packet.

It is fun to read about vegetables in seed catalogs. The virtues of the plants may be somewhat exaggerated, but the growing characteristics can be trusted as described. Look for varieties that are native to our area. These will be hardier and more disease resistant. With high quality seeds, there is no need to plant multiple seeds and thin later, since each seed will do well. An excellent source of tomato seeds is the heirloom tomatoes that you eat. If you find one that is particularly tasty, save the seeds. The general rule of thumb for planting any seed is to plant it four times as deep as the size of the seed.

Vegetables that are easy to grow from seeds planted directly in the garden include beets, bok choy, carrots, chard, collards, corn, cucumbers, green beans, kale, lettuce, lima beans, melons, okra, peas, squash, spinach, spring onions, turnips and zucchini. All of these sprout quite rapidly.

Vegetables that you may prefer to purchase (or grow) as seedlings for transplant include tomatoes, peppers, and eggplants. Asparagus and rutabaga are best purchased as roots.

Extending your growing season

Vegetable gardening is not just for the spring or the summer. With the right protection, you can start before the last frost, then garden well into the fall and even through the dead of winter.

Tomatoes stop growing once it gets hot, so planting early is desirable. To keep them from freezing if you plant before May 15, surround them by a "Wall of Water" (very inexpensive on Amazon.com). With this insulation system, you can plant as early as mid-March.

Another way to get a head start on spring planting is to buy small seedlings in the early spring but then keep them in a cold frame (which is like a miniature greenhouse) until safely past the last frost, re-potting them as they grow. You can buy commercial cold frames or else make one using an old storm window or clear plastic.

At the other end of the season, there are all sorts of ways to keep the garden going even into the dead of winter. Some plants that will keep on growing if protected are chard, mustard greens and Red Russian kale. The simplest method is to cover your garden with insulating grower's cloth. This can work for plants that stay short, such as lettuce and radishes. Insulating cloth comes in various thicknesses: the thicker the cloth, the better the insulation, but the less sunlight it will let through. You will be amazed to find crops growing even under the snow.
For taller plants, such as beets and carrots, install arching brackets over your garden (available from Gardener's Supply Company) and lay the cloth on top of that to form a tunnel. Weigh down the edges to keep it from blowing away.

Greenhouses in all shapes, sizes and price ranges can be purchased from large hardware stores. Slightly more elaborate is the "Grow Camp" greenhouse. This 4 foot tall greenhouse has a raised bed, heavy plastic curtains that roll up, and netting for keeping off the bugs in the summer. It is easy to use because the plants are held up off the ground.

A real greenhouse requires a lot of attention to detail to succeed. The temperature needs to be controlled (around 66 degrees seems to work) and also the humidity. Commercial green houses have exhaust fans controlled by humistats, which you can use as well. The concept that plants need specific UV light spectra and therefore special light bulbs is disputed; some say a regular floursecent bulb will work fine.

Weeds

Weeding is a sad necessity in a vegetable garden. If you mulch the garden very heavily, it will keep down the weeds, and you may find that you do not need to water very much. If you are using straw for mulch, put down newspaper underneath to keep its seeds from germinating. Alternatively, you can lay down landscape cloth between the rows. Covering your beds in the winter with a thick layer of straw or a tarp will keep weed seeds from blowing in.

Some weeds, such as perslane and dandelions, can continue to go to seed even after you uproot them, so do not leave them lying in your garden.

Feeding your plants

There is quite a variety of opinion among our contributors about how much to feed vegetables, ranging from "Fertilize vegetable gardens generously" to "Feed them, but don't overfeed them: one application of slow release fertilizer at the beginning should be enough" to "Fertilize sparingly." One simple approach is to fertilize everything once a year with 10-10-10. For acid loving plants, add granular sulfur to lower the pH.

There is a saying among organic gardeners that you should "feed the soil, not the plant." In other words, if you add enough compost to your soil, fertilizer becomes largely unnecessary. Vegetables are different from shrubs and trees. Vegetables are generally annuals, and their yield is harvested every year, or sometimes multiple times a year. Vegetables are healthy because they contain lots of nutrients, which they get from the soil. So every time you pick a tomato or pepper, you are in effect taking nutrients from the soil and transferring them to your own body. You can replace these lost nutrients with fertilizers or compost. Compost builds up the soil biologically and structurally, but fertilizers have their role as sort of a last resort amendment. If your plants are growing noticeably poorly, and it's not a result of heat, deer or other pests, fertilizers are a good option to get a quick boost of nutrients to correct the poor growth. However, for general maintenance of the soil from year to year, compost is best.

One of the easiest ways to add compost is to place it as a thin mulch right on the surface of the garden bed – no tilling needed. If you are putting in transplants, you can also add a handful of compost with each hole you dig. Compost builds up soil structure over time, and tilling can sometimes break up those nice soil aggregates that you are slowly forming. Mulching avoids this and involves a lot less labor.

The best way to tell if your soil is deficient in any nutrient is to get a soil test from the Virginia Cooperative Extension. The test costs $10 and you get the results back in about a week. Test kits can be picked up at public libraries.

For a vegetable garden, an excellent fertilizer is two year old (or older) horse manure if you can find it. Be careful not to use manure that is too young (not "cured") because it will burn your vegetables and prevent germination. Another excellent alternative to slow release chemical fertilizers is Chickity Doo Doo, which is pelletized chicken manure. Its nitrogen content of five percent is far higher than other kinds of manure. It also contains 9% calcium.

Bugs

Some vegetables, such as cabbage, are difficult to grow without using massive amount of pesticide to control the caterpillars. Why bother to grow a vegetable if you have to apply a pesticide to the part you eat? Eggplants need to be sprayed with Sevin in the spring; cucumbers must be sprayed in summer to kill the cucumber bugs.

You can get around one of these problems by waiting until July to sow vines such as squash and cucumbers. The squash vine borer caterpillar turns into a butterfly by then and won't eat your plants after that. Squash likes hot weather, so planting in July is not a problem. If you want to plant earlier than July, separate the vines in your garden, because if you put them together, they will attract more insects.

You can fight fire with fire by buying praying mantis egg cases and welcoming these little natural guardians to your garden. Ladybugs need to be put out at night or they will fly away immediately - and even then, most of them will leave - but praying mantises will stay.

Slugs can be thoroughly foiled by copper wire. Affix a band of adhesive copper tape around the outside of your raised bed or other container: slugs absolutely won't cross it, as it gives them a little static shock.

Bigger animals

Bird netting is generally not a good solution for bird problems. Birds can get trapped in the net. Other animals get tangled in it and make a mess. Your weed whacker and lawn mower get caught in it, and you have to lift it up to work under it, which becomes progressively more of a nuisance as your plants grow up through it. Building a large frame to hold it up and out does solve some of these difficulties.

A better solution for birds is to buy "bird tape," an iridescent shiny ribbon which sparkles in the sun and scares away the birds. It really works! Stretch it out between tall stakes, stringing it right above your plants and twisting it as you go.

Be prepared for major crop destruction if you do not have a good fence to keep out the deer, raccoons, rabbits, etc. Crows will eat the corn as soon as the seedlings emerge, so you need to cover it for the first month. As soon as the ear develops, squirrels and raccoons take over from the crows. To keep the raccoons from eating your corn, you can cover each ear with a plastic grocery bag, holding it on with a loose rubber band. More effective, though, is a motion triggered water squirter (available on line and in some garden centers), which zaps them when they are up to 20 feet away and keeps on zapping until they are gone. They hate it!

Two plant crops that are safe from deer are onions and garlic. You can plant large numbers in September or October and get a good crop the next year, and no fence is needed.

Tips for specific crops

What follows is not an exhaustive manual on growing produce, but rather our contributors' favorite tips.

Tomatoes

The biggest mistake beginners make is to give them too much water, which will cause the roots to deteriorate and the leaves to yellow. Water them only when the soil starts to dry out.

You should not need pesticides on tomatoes, but they are susceptible to cutworms. The usual way to control cutworms is to create a collar (such as an empty tomato paste can or a paper cup with the bottom cut out) and press it ¼ inch into the ground, leaving about 1½ inches above the surface. Of course, squirrels and rabbits may still nibble on the growing tomatoes.

Tomatoes are prone to "blossom end rot," in which the bottom of the tomato turns black and then the whole tomato rots. This can be prevented with a small addition of lime to the soil, which provides the calcium needed to prevent end rot. Eggshells are often used but take too long to dissolve. The calcium in lime is more readily available. Bone meal (also used) is not as water soluble as lime.

Tomato cages are more expensive than stakes but easier to use and can easily be reused year after year. When growing tomatoes in a container, you need to put in fresh soil every year, at least around where the roots will be. In the garden, rotate the location from year to year.

Berries

Black and red *raspberries, blueberries,* and *gooseberries* are all options in our climate. Black raspberries are particularly hardy and tolerant. Blueberries and gooseberries have very shallow root systems, so you can even take them with you if you move! Do not buy wineberries, however tasty. They are invasive aliens.

Raspberries (both red and black), require a raised bed. Planted in the open, they sprawl everywhere in an unkempt mess, making it difficult to weed and impossible to mow between plants. To double your yield and keep them tidier, tie each cluster to a nine foot stake. You will get more fruit if canes are not sprawling on the ground with leaves covering them, and it is easier to work with them when they are neatly bundled. Stick a rebar in each corner of your raised bed and then string a wire around in a rectangle to lend added support. To get three harvests per season, cut each cane to the ground after it finishes producing. The mid-summer harvest will not be as big as the spring and fall harvest but will still be worth having. There is a thornless variety of black raspberries, but it is not as tasty.

Other crops

Asparagus is a very easy crop to grow. It is a perennial plant. The first year, harvest only the first two weeks. Year two, harvest for four weeks. After that, harvest for six weeks. Stop harvesting at the end of May, then let it grow naturally to replenish the plant. Plant eighteen inches apart. Asparagus gets very weedy. One way to prevent that is to cover it with landscape cloth in October. If you have access to manure, pile 4-5 inches on top of the landscape cloth. The nutrients will leach through the cloth and feed the asparagus, resulting in an earlier crop. Remove the manure in the spring. Asparagus (as does *rhubarb*) requires extremely porous soil. Mix ⅔ sand with ⅓ soil.

Corn requires a lot of room. Don't grow popcorn with sweet corn, since the cross pollination will ruin both varieties. If you get stunted ears of corn, you always can dry them out and grind them into corn flour.

Garlic is easy to grow. Buy the hard neck type for this climate. Garlic can be planted in your flower garden. There are hundreds of types, with different tastes. Some are mild, some hot and spicy, some have more bite. Save the biggest for seeds for next time. When you pull it up, little baby garlics are left behind and will come up the next year.

Green beans should not be planted too deep. Plant two crops, three weeks apart in the spring. Pole beans are less susceptible to insects than bush beans, because they are further from the ground. Fortex green beans grow 10-12 feet high and have beans that are almost a foot long. You can train them up a tall stake then let them grow down the other side. Sow beans directly in the ground since they do not transplant well.

Onions are not generally started from seeds. You can buy 100 presprouted plants for around $8 from the Vermont Bean Seed company. Onions must be kept absolutely clear of weeds and given adequate fertilizer. The depth determines whether you get an onion bulb or just leaves. Don't plant more than 1 inch deep. Be careful which variety you buy. Vidalia onions are mild, but others may leave tears streaming down your face.

Potatoes ultimately should be six or seven inches underground, but if you plant them that deep initially, they will not make it to the surface. So plant shallower and add dirt on top as they sprout.

Swiss chard is an under-appreciated plant that is easy to grow and delicious to eat. It lasts all summer and into the fall and may even winter over. There are several kinds of Swiss chard: red stems, yellow stems and green stems. They all are great and healthy foods and beautiful plants. You will not need many of them, as they put out more leaves than one family can eat, so you will be able to share them with neighbors.

Yams actually require poor soil. Unimproved clay is just right for them. They take a lot of space in the garden.

Fruit trees

Unfortunately, fruit trees are not known for longevity, and if you want to have picture perfect fruit, you will need to do a lot of spraying. This is harmful for the environment and a lot of work. An exception is certain apple trees. They live a little longer and are much hardier and disease resistant. The Cox's Orange Pippin variety yields extremely tasty apples, if not necessarily the most beautiful. Very little care is needed if you are willing to simply cut out the worms. After all, if it is safe for the worm to eat, it is safe for us to eat, too!

Blueberries 101

Those pots of blueberry plants that show up in front of grocery stores each spring are so tempting, and what could be better than having a ready supply of berries right in your own yard? But if you don't follow a few simple rules, those plants will be gone in a matter of months, or, if they survive, will remain stubbornly fruitless.

Here's what you need to successfully grow blueberries in Northern Virginia:

1. At least two blueberry plants, *of different varieties*, for cross-pollination. Check the labels on the pots. They will tell you the name of each variety as well as its characteristics. Do you want small, tart berries, or big, sweet ones?

2. Soil acidifier. The soil here is too alkaline for blueberries, so each year, you will need to acidify it to the berries' liking. Your two basic choices are aluminum sulfate or an organic-based sulfate (Epoma is a good brand). Aluminum sulfate will work faster but should only be used once to avoid toxifying the soil. Organic-based sulfates release more slowly but are both safe for continued use and appropriate for organic growing.

3. A pH kit. This is a simple and inexpensive kit, available at garden and home improvement stores, which will tell you whether your soil is acid enough. Blueberries prefer a soil acidity of 4.5-5.0. pH meters are not as reliable.

4. Patience! You will not be able to harvest your berries until the second year, and even then you should only take very small amounts. The shrubs will readily fruit if allowed, but you should remove the budding berries so the plant will apply more energy to growing its branches and greenery. This will encourage maximum growth, which in turn will lead to larger harvests of better berries. Berries from newly planted or poorly established shrubs tend to be small, bitter and dry.

Once you have all of your supplies assembled, plant the shrubs according to the instructions on the labels. Blueberries have a shallow root system and will do very nicely in the ground or in raised beds. If planting in the ground, be sure to dig a hole that is both deep and wide enough. Try to choose a location with plenty of morning and early afternoon sun. Full sun all day is fine, but bushes that are planted in intense, direct afternoon sun will need more frequent watering. Blueberry shrubs are deciduous, so the foliage will change color and then drop in the fall. This may be a factor in determining where you want to plant your bushes.

After the shrubs are planted, evenly apply your soil acidifier in a wide circle from the plant's base to the drip line (where water will run off the leaves onto the ground). Be generous: it takes quite a bit to properly acidify the soil. Water the shrubs thoroughly, and then test the pH. Add more acidifier if necessary. If the soil is too acid, lime can be used to increase the pH, but making the soil too acidic for blueberries is rarely a problem. Apply a thin layer of mulch and, if desired, landscape fabric to cut down on weeds.

Be sure to keep your newly installed plants watered, and remember that you'll need to reapply soil acidifier and a good fertilizer each year. Blueberry shrubs that have been well-cared for will exceed six feet in height and yield many gallons of berries per season.

Once your shrubs begin to yield nicely sized crops (typically in the third year), you'll likely find that bird netting is necessary to protect your harvest. An important harvesting tip: pull the berries gently. If they don't easily come off the branch, they aren't quite ripe. Blueberries at peak ripeness will easily fall off with light pressure.

This may seem like a complicated process, but it really is very simple and much less expensive than purchasing cartons of berries from the store. Once you see your huge, thriving shrubs, you're sure to enjoy a wonderful sense of accomplishment!

Finally, if you do lose a blueberry bush (most commonly due to inadequate watering), don't give up on it! A bare plant that seems dead and gone in the summer or fall may still fully revive in the spring. Just keep watering.

Why go organic?

The chemicals we put on our lawns and gardens end up in our water and in the stomachs of the birds, animals, and fish that share our habitat. Good gardeners consider not just the immediate gratification of flowers and lawn, but their impact on the soil and the world around them.

Clearly, the bulk of the ongoing damage to our environment comes not from home gardens but from buildings and other construction, industry and agriculture. So why even worry about the impact of our little gardens? Our home is one place where we can in fact control our actions and live a life consistent with our principles. Trying to garden organically fosters an awareness of the destructiveness of our species and may influence our other choices which can have a wider impact. Even our own small gardens are important to the individual plants and animals that make them their home. And if large numbers of Northern Virginians change their gardening habits, it really will make a substantial impact on our local environment.

When English Quaker Joseph Hoag was pleading his peace principles in 1812, a man in his audience said, "Well stranger, if all the world was of your mind, I would turn and follow after." Joseph replied, "So then thou hast a mind to be the last man in the world to be good. I have a mind to be one of the first and set the rest an example."

There are whole books on how to garden without damaging the environment, but here are a few highlights:

Grow the soil

Serious gardeners who want lasting results spend their efforts first and foremost on soil improvement. Composting is *de rigueur.*

Organic products *vs.* harmful chemicals

For every chemical product that you use for fertilizer, weed killer, pesticide or fungicide, there is an alternative product or gardening technique available. For best results, though, you need to plan ahead, since many of these techniques only yield results over a much longer period of time.

Healthy plants resist disease

A plant that is well suited to its environment will naturally need less care. Organic gardeners try to avoid chemicals altogether, even organic ones, if they can. Flower gardens in particular can do just fine without any applications other than compost. When necessary, though, fertilizing will result in sturdier plants.

Pest control

Diversity of planting attracts the diversity of wildlife – insects, birds and small mammals – that will create a natural balance and help prevent infestations. Clear away rubbish, weeds and cuttings because they attract fungi and insects. Companion planting - using some plants specifically to control pests and diseases - works by either repelling bugs by the smell (marigolds, certain herbs) or by attracting beneficial insects (for example, yarrow (*Achillea)* attracts hover flies which eat aphids).

It should go without saying that since one of the reasons we grow native plants is to feed the insects, then it is okay to let the insects eat the plants. Generally speaking, native insects will not eat more than 20% of a plant. There are a few exceptions, but even those are not harmful in the long run. For instance, the tent caterpillar will strip the leaves off a cherry tree, but then new leaves will sprout and the tree remains unharmed. The two evolved together and are meant to function that way.

Crop rotation

Moving vegetables around from year to year cuts down on diseases. It is critical to the success of truck gardening.

Water conservation

The term "xeriscaping" refers to landscaping that is designed to use as little water as possible. Techniques include using plants with low water requirements, avoiding grass in impractical areas, mulching and using drip irrigation systems or soaker hoses rather than sprinklers.

Clipping hedges

If you have a bush that has to be kept trimmed, here are some basic rules:

- Buy an electric hedge clipper. It is well worth the investment.
- Never let a bush grow taller than you can reach. Pruning from a ladder is even less fun than pruning from the ground.
- The base should be wider than the top. If the top is wider, it will shade out the lower branches, and snow will bend it out of shape.
- Never let any bush overgrow the walkway.
- Most important rule: buy a bush that when full grown will be the right size for the space, so you never have to prune! It is very difficult to keep a formal hedge in shape long term, and an asymmetrical formal hedge is likely to look pretty sad.

Container gardening

Those gorgeous hanging plants at the garden centers don't always stay gorgeous for long. They are sold when at their most beautiful but within a very few weeks start to get gangly. Be sure to add some time-release fertilizer. Regular pruning and dead heading will encourage thicker growth.

Maintaining both moisture and drainage are the big challenges in containers. For that reason, the bigger, the better. Moss-lined wire baskets don't last long and dry out very quickly, requiring frequent watering. On the other end of the spectrum, cast iron pots with no drain holes quickly become waterlogged. Ceramic pots are beautiful but heavy and may crack in the winter. Composite plastics are the most popular, and if you don't like the color, you can often spray paint them.

Flowering plants packed into the small space of a hanging planter often have a tremendous water requirement. Even if you have the time and desire to water once or twice a day, one late day at work on a ninety degree day may spell the end of your carefully tended pot. To get around this, buy self-watering hanging pots and fill them yourself with plants with lower water requirements. "Self-watering" planters have a reservoir at the bottom which you fill through a hole. Even these may need refilling every day or two in the very hottest weather.

Containers are ideal for valuable but very invasive plants, such as mint.

A few suggestions for successful container plants in our climate

Shade annuals
Coleus (the tall ones may tolerate some sun), fuschia (dappled shade), impatiens, begonias (these can be overwintered in your house), creeping Jenny (this is an invasive plant so should not go into the ground nor be allowed to go to seed).

Shade perennials
Japanese forest grass, forget-me-nots (*Brunnera macrophylla* 'Jack Frost' - evergreen variegated heart shaped leaves).

Sun annuals
Geraniums (may be overwintered in your house), lantanas, petunias (these need a lot of trimming to keep them from getting leggy), dusty miller (may even overwinter outdoors), marigolds, mandevilla (use a small trellis for this vine).

Sun perennials
Sedum, thyme, rosemary, sago palm, hardy hibiscus, chrysanthemums.

Cutting gardens

If you love to bring in cut flowers, you can dedicate a part of your garden for that purpose, perhaps in an area that does not show as much but where you can easily water. Here you can plant flowers closer together than you ordinarily would, since you will be cutting them back regularly.

Some flowers that do well when cut include:

Bulbs/tubers
    allium
    crocosmia
    dahlias
    daffodils
    gladiolus

Annuals
    coleus
    cosmos
    marigolds
    sunflowers
    zinnias

Perennials
    asters
    bee balm
    chrysanthemums
    hellebore
    lilies
    peonies
    purple coneflower
    Russian sage
    yarrow

And of course some shrubs are great for cutting, including roses, forsythia, lilacs and hydrangeas. Forsythia (among other shrubs) can be forced to bloom in February if you cut them and put them in water inside. If you can bring yourself to cut off one of the blooms, a rhododendron flower with a little foliage makes for a showy and long-lasting centerpiece. *Magnolia grandiflora* clippings work well for holiday decorating.

Southern Magnolia

Roses

Tea roses make gorgeous cut flowers, but they require a lot of work. Left to themselves, hordes of Japanese beetles make mincemeat out of any leaves that are spared by black spot. You can spray your roses frequently and try to cut down on the Japanese beetle population (milky spore is the most effective control method for those but will not eliminate them by any means). Or you can buy Knock Out roses, which bloom longer and more profusely than tea roses without any of the heartbreak (but without much fragrance, either). Other relatively disease resistant roses are also available, which you can look up on the web.

Care of tea roses
The basic care of tea roses starts with pruning around St Patrick's Day. Make your cut immediately above a bud that is pointing away from the center of the bush. That way, the new sprouts will grow outwards, and the center will get enough light and air circulation. Paint the pruned ends with white glue or tree pitch to keep the borer caterpillar from attacking the ends. If the center ends up too crowded, remove a few leaves if necessary. Remove yellow leaves or any with black spot.

If you really want to maximize your success, spray the bush once every 4-6 weeks with a 3-in-1 spray (insecticide, miticide and fungicide) and fertilize throughout the growing season. This is obviously very bad for the local insect population.

To prevent black spot, the leaves of roses need to be kept dry. Yet roses need a lot of water. So water in the morning, when there is time for them to dry out by nightfall, and preferably use a soaker hose to avoid getting water on the leaves altogether.

Sometimes the root stock takes over and you get a different color bloom. Hybrid tea roses are grafted on a root stock which has been selected for being hardy. If the grafted portion of the plant dies, a different – and likely less attractive – rose will take over.

Knock Out roses
Knock Out roses are a type of shrub rose. Unlike tea roses, you do not prune back the entire bush every year. Rather, don't prune it at all the first two or three years (unless necessary for shaping) and after that cut out one third of the canes at the base (leaving the younger canes). Spraying and fertilizing are unnecessary.

Lawn care

How much imperfection can you tolerate? There is nothing even remotely natural about growing a lawn this far south and with our soil conditions. Most turf grass originally comes from alpine areas of Europe – clearly a very different environment from the D.C. area. As a result, it browns up during our hot summers but grows like crazy during the cool early spring. To achieve a perfect lawn requires applying large amounts of water, lime, fertilizers, herbicide and pesticides. All this takes a lot of work and damages our environment, as do the emissions from power lawn mowers and leaf blowers

Grass prefers a pH right around 7 (neutral), while most soils here are in the 5-6.5 pH range. If you are trying to grow trees in your grass, this can be troublesome. The native trees like their native acidic soils, while the grass wants a higher pH. If you lime the soil to raise the pH, it helps the grass but hurts the trees. It is best to create planter beds for trees and shrubs that are free of grass so they won't have to compete.

The simplest approach to lawn maintenance includes putting down pre-emergence crabgrass killer in the early spring (before the dandelions reach the puffball stage) and spreading new grass seed and fertilizer after Labor Day. Lime is usually needed every few years to raise the pH. You need to remove leaves from the lawn so it does not get smothered, although chopped leaves can be left in place to feed the soil - as can grass clippings - if the piles are not too thick. The Virginia Cooperative Extension has numerous documents available with everything you need to know to have a successful lawn. If you hire a lawn service, the contract may automatically include large quantities of chemicals, whether you need them or not, but the results are obviously very professional looking.

If you want your lawn to stay green all summer, you will need to water it in dry weather. Otherwise, during extended droughts, the grass will go dormant but green up again when the rains start. Don't cut your grass when the temperature is over 90 degrees. The most commonly used turf grasses, such as fescue, are cool weather plants which stop growing in the heat. If you mow the grass then, the blades will no longer be shading the roots, and the plant will be very stressed.

Before putting down seed, it is a very good idea to aerate the lawn. You can buy an inexpensive plug aerator to drag behind your mower. Weigh it down with concrete blocks, and do the aerating after a rain or watering softens the ground. You can also rent aerators. Spike aerators are not effective.

One of the problems with lawns is that they are usually grown on clay that was dug out for the foundation of the house and which is missing its topsoil. Adding organic material such as Milorganite or Nutri-Green (both of which are made from sewage sludge) will improve the soil, providing nutrients and reducing compaction. You can rent a compost spreader or just empty out the bags and rake it out.

If you think of a lawn as simply a flat green space that can be walked on, it opens up other possibilities besides grass. Violets and clover, for instance, are native plants which spread naturally and fulfill the purpose of a lawn quite nicely. Ultimately, if you do nothing at all to your lawn other than mowing it, the perennial grass will gradually be replaced by a mixture of moss and annual plants, which will include some grass and some broad-leaf weeds. It will be adequately green in the summer and a nice light brown in the winter. Perhaps you will decide that brown is a perfectly acceptable winter color for a field!

If you decide to reduce the size of your lawn, you will want to do more than simply stop mowing, because most likely the lawn will be overrun by invasive alien plants rather than revert to native woods. Give nature a hand by planting meadow plants (if you have enough sun), ground-covers or trees.

You may be wondering why other people have lawns that have individual blades of grass, while your grass blades have branches. If so, it is because your lawn (and probably your garden) has been overrun by Japanese stilt grass, an invasive which has taken over in Northern Virginia in the past few years. It is an annual grass which can be partly controlled in the lawn with pre-emergence crabgrass killer. Outside of the lawn, the most effective approach is to pull it up by hand before it goes to seed in September. It is very easy to tear up from the ground.

Growing from seeds

Starting plants from seeds is fun, but you must provide enough warmth and light and protect against fungi.

When starting seeds indoors, you can warm the pots on top of your hot water heater, and then put them in a sunny window when they start to sprout. However, windows may be drafty and their sunlight unreliable. A common alternative is to put the seedlings under a light for 12 hours or more per day. Fluorescent lights are best. There is no need to buy more expensive "grow lights," which have a blue-red tinge simply to make the plants look nicer under the light. Rather, mix 40 watt warm white with cool white or daylight bulbs. They should be hung a few inches above the seedlings and raised as the seedlings grow.

Seeds and seedlings can be killed by a variety of fungi, collectively known as damping-off disease. You therefore should not re-use potting soil for growing seeds nor use soil brought in from outdoors. You can buy products to spray on to prevent fungi, but an easier method is to use seed starter kits, which are simply plastic trays with either 24 or 72 compacted peat moss compartments. The compartments expand when sufficient water is added to the tray. It is better to use a new starter kit each year.

People who prefer the do-it-yourself approach have these suggestions:
- Re-use plastic pots and sterilize them by soaking them in diluted Clorox (about one cup in five gallons of water).

- Or cut a slit in the bottom of paper or plastic cups for drainage, and fill with Miracle Grow potting soil. (To save money and the environment, you can reuse discarded cups.)
- For tiny seeds, such as parsley or basil, you can use take-out food containers covered with plastic wrap until they sprout.

Even if the last week in April feels like summer, there is likely to be a cool spell in the middle of May. If you intend to move your plants outdoors in mid-May, plant the seeds at the end of March or the beginning of April. "Harden" your plants by exposing them to the outside sunlight and temperature for a couple of hours the first day and a couple of hours more each day thereafter.

Not all seeds can be easily sown directly in the garden, but some do perform well, including zinnias, marigolds, cleome, nasturtiums, cosmos, and most vegetables. In fact, tall plants such as cleome and cosmos may tend to fall over when transplanted, so growing directly from seeds is actually better. Larkspur and poppies can be spread in December. Be sure you are planting in dirt and not in mulch. When planting outdoors, you have the same problem as Mother Nature: only a small percentage of the seed you put out will germinate and survive. The yield is much higher when you start seeds indoors under controlled conditions.

Home gardeners usually do not grow perennials from seeds, because most perennials do not bloom their first year.

Moist conditions will seriously reduce germination rates. Leftover seeds that are stored in a cool, dry place may germinate the next year, but the yield will be lower

.

Herbs

Most herbs originated in the Mediterranean and therefore like it dry and hot. Herbs can be scattered in your garden to add interesting leaf colors and texture. They also make an attractive edging or can serve as a ground cover in sunny locations. And a formal herb garden is a very elegant sight.

Sage, thyme, oregano, chives, savory and many other herbs make great perennials. They come back year after year and provide you with fresh herbs to use in your cooking all year round. Rosemary may or may not make it through the winter here.

Italian, or flat leaf, parsley is slower to grow than curly parsley but gets very lush and comes back the next spring. You can also bring containers of parsley into your garage in the winter where they will keep on producing as long as they get some light. Parsley is biennial.

Basil is strictly annual but generally quite successful. Unfortunately, in this climate, dill, cilantro and lemon grass are difficult to grow.

The best location for an herb garden is right next to your kitchen door, where you can enjoy the aroma and have easy access for cooking.

Poison ivy

Poison ivy is a beneficial native plant, so we should not be trying to exterminate it. It provides food for birds in winter when other food is scarce. However, it makes a very poor garden plant. You can eradicate it fairly effectively from your yard with weed killer. Round Up is thought to be safe for the environment unless it gets into water, at which point it is highly toxic to frogs. Round Up Pro is more expensive but safe for the frogs.

Don't just look down to spot poison ivy. Many a poison ivy vine has climbed up into trees and bushes and created a veritable bush of its own. You may suddenly realize that the tree you are standing under is not a tree after all! The vines climbing on trees have a hairy appearance. Do not touch those vines! Cut them at the ground and spray with weed killer. Do not attempt to pull out the weeds by hand, no matter how much you cover yourself up first.

You don't need to have poison ivy growing in your own yard to be exposed. Bags of mulch and leaf mold may have poison ivy mixed in. At least wear gloves when handling mulch and consider wearing long sleeves, long pants and socks. You can also rub on pre-contact treatments that help prevent the rash. Be careful not to burn poison ivy. The smoke can cause a severe rash, even in your eyes, nose and mouth.

If you know you were exposed to poison ivy, you can wash with Tecnu or other products to neutralize the oil. Wash all clothes that may have been exposed, including gloves and tools (and house pets, who will be unaffected themselves but who may bring you an unwelcome present).

Poison ivy allergies can be quite serious for some people. For anyone in that category, the safest thing to do is to get a landscaper to eradicate it for you.

Poison ivy

Reliable perennials for our climate

What follows is a list of perennials recommended by our contributors because they grow successfully in Northern Virginia. The list is intended to be a handy reference to quickly look up whether or not a given plant is native or deer resistant (you can also use the index for that) and the basic growing conditions.

The term "perennial" is a little confusing. In charts such as the one that follows, "perennial" refers to anything that is not annual. But the term is also used more specifically to refer to "herbaceous perennials," a plant that dies back to the ground in the winter then reemerges on the same roots in the spring.

This list does not include those plants which are a threat to the environment in Virginia because they are invasive aliens. All of those will grow here reliably as well - only too reliably! See their separate list, and please don't plant them. The list also does not include any alien ornamental grass or ground-covers. Although only a few are officially designated as a threat in Virginia, their great potential to spread makes them quite worrisome. Instead, the list includes a number of native grasses and ground-covers which make good alternatives. If some of these native plants with inconspicuous flowers seem pointless to you when you see them as individual specimens, most likely their aesthetic value in gardens would be as a mass planting.

For purposes of this chart, "native" is defined quite loosely to include plants that are indigenous to nearby areas but not necessarily to the Potomac Valley.

There is no attempt to separate "part sun," "part shade," "dappled shade," "light shade," *etc..* All are simply listed as "part sun." In fact, many other details had to be left out of the chart because of space limitations. It is always a good idea to read more about plants before you buy them. For example, hostas do best when provided with morning sun but protected from the afternoon sun; they will survive under the opposite conditions but look a little parched.

Where the notation for moisture requirement is left blank, assume that the plant has the usual requirements: regular watering for the first year or until it is established (trees take two or three years to become established), then only in times of drought. Some of the native plants for which the moisture column was left blank may actually be fine with drought – most natives are.

Bloom time can vary from year to year and even from one end of a street to another. It must be very nerve wracking to grow your own wedding flowers, as some people do, and be on a deadline!

The notations for deer resistance are only intended to give you a general idea, as a very hungry deer will not follow the rules. Young trees can be protected by a wire enclosure until their branches grow out of reach, as can tall shrubs. Many plants will survive being pruned by deer but will have no blossoms.

Very possibly, some of your favorites are missing. If so, and assuming they are not on the "Do Not Plant" list, please send an email to takeouradvice@takeouradvice.org.

Abbreviations:

○	Full Sun
◐	Part Sun/Shade
●	Shade
spp.	species

Many plants have more than one sun symbol listed, because they are open-minded and tolerate varying degrees of sun exposure.

Balloon
Flower

Reliable perennials list

Scientific name	Common name	Light	Moisture	Bloom time	Comments	Native?	Type	Deer resistant?
Abelia spp.	abelia	○ ◐		summer		no	shrub	yes
Acer palmatum	Japanese maple				Hundreds of cultivars, with different growing conditions.	no	tree	yes
Achillea spp.	yarrow	○	Drought tolerant	summer	Looks best in a mass planting.	some	perennial	yes
Adiantum pedatum	northern maidenhead fern	◐ ●			Interesting fronds held up in the air on a little post.	yes	fern	yes
Aesculus parviflora	bottlebrush buckeye	○ ◐ ●	Drought tolerant	June	Gets very large and magnificent. Needs some sun to bloom. Cannot tolerate wet feet.	yes	shrub	yes
Allium spp.	allium, ornamental onions	○			Balls of flowers on a spike. Many species.	some	bulbs	yes
Amelanchier canadensis	serviceberry, shadbush	○ ◐ ●	Drought and wet tolerant	April	Lots of white flowers, edible fruit.	yes	tree	yes
Amsonia spp.	bluestar	○ ◐	Drought tolerant	spring		yes	perennial	yes
Aquilegia	columbine	○ ◐	Drought tolerant	June	Nodding flowers.	some	perennial	yes
Arisaema	Jack-in-the-pulpit	●		spring		yes	perennial	?

Scientific name	Common name	Light	Moisture	Bloom time	Comments	Native?	Type	Deer resistant?
Aronia arbutifolia 'Brilliantisma'	red chokeberry	○ ◐		spring		yes	shrub	?
Asarum canadense	wild ginger	◐ ●	Drought and wet tolerant		Ground-cover. Tolerates deep shade.	yes	perennial	yes
Asclepias tuberosa	butterfly weed	○ ◐	Drought and wet tolerant	June	Butterflies love it.	yes	perennial	yes
Astilbe spp.	astilbe, false spirea, false goat's beard, feather flower	○ ◐ ●		May-July	Feathery flowers.	no	perennial	yes
Baptisia australis	blue false indigo	○ ◐	Drought tolerant	spring	Leaves like clover, small purple flowers. Very hard to remove.	yes	perennial	yes
Bignonia capreolata	cross-vine	○ ◐		spring	Spring blooms, 2 inch pink or red flowers.	yes	vine	yes
Bletilla spp.	hardy orchid	●	Drought tolerant	spring		no	perennial	yes
Brunnera macrophylla 'Jack Frost'	Siberian bugloss	◐		early spring	Variegated leaves with blue forget-me-not flowers in spring. Heat tolerant. Like small hosta, only better!	no	perennial	yes
Buxus spp.	boxwood	○ ◐				no	shrub	yes
Calycanthus spp.	sweetshrub	○ ◐		spring	Fragrant flowers. 'Venus and' 'Athens' cultivars are good.	yes	shrub	yes

147

Scientific name	Common name	Light	Moisture	Bloom time	Comments	Native?	Type	Deer resistant?
Camellia spp.	camellia	◐		early spring or late fall		no	shrub	yes
Caryopteris spp.	bluebeard	○		summer		no	shrub	yes
Cephalanthus occidentalis	buttonbush	○ ◐	Wet tolerant		Cute white button flowers. Attracts butterflies.	yes	shrub	yes
Cephalotaxus harringtonia	Japanese plum yew	○ ◐ ●	Drought tolerant		Evergreen.	no	shrub	yes
Cercis canadensis	redbud, eastern redbud	○ ◐		April	Lovely purple flowers. These trees dot wood edges.	yes	tree	no
Chasmanthium latifolia	sea oats	○			Great seed heads. Can be aggressive.	yes	grass	yes
Cheloni lyonii	pink turtlehead	○ ◐	Wet tolerant	summer		yes	perennial	?
Chionanthus virginicus	fringe tree	○ ◐		spring	Lovely white flowers.	yes	tree	?
Chionodoxa spp.	glory-of-the-snow	○ ◐	Drought tolerant	March	Carpet of blue flowers under trees.	no	bulb	yes
Chrysanthemum spp.	chrysanthemum	○		July - Nov	Blooms most of the summer but especially in the fall. Avoid florist mums which are less hardy.	no	perennial	no
Chrysogonum virginianum	green and gold	◐		early spring	Tiny plant with yellow flowers.	yes	perennial	yes

Reliable perennials list

Scientific name	Common name	Light	Moisture	Bloom time	Comments	Native?	Type	Deer resistant?
Cimicifuga racemosa	black cohosh, snakeroot	●	Drought tolerant	July	Tall white flower spires tower over the foliage.	yes	perennial	yes
Clethra anilfolia	summersweet	○ ◐ ●	Wet tolerant	Aug	Bees love it.	yes	shrub	yes
Coreopsis verticillata 'Moonbeam'	threadleaf coreopsis 'Moonbeam'	○	Drought tolerant	June	Mound shape with yellow flowers. Long blooming, very reliable.	yes	perennial	yes
Cornus racemosa	northern swamp dogwood, gray dogwood	○ ◐ ●	Drought and wet tolerant		Birds love the fruit.	yes	shrub	?
Cornus sericea	redtwig dogwood, red osier dogwood	○ ◐ ●	Wet tolerant		Red twigs (or yellow in the case of the 'Flaviramea' variety) lend winter interest.	yes	shrub	yes
Crocosmia spp.	crocosmia	○		summer	Tall red flowers. Avoid crocosmia x crocosmiiflora, which is invasive.	no	bulbs	yes
Crocus	crocus	○ ◐ ●		March	Animals may eat them, but if you plant a lot, you will still get a lot.	no	bulbs	yes
Cyclamen hederifolium	hardy cyclamen	●	Drought tolerant	fall		no	perennial	yes
Dennstaedia punctilobula	hayscented fern	◐	Drought tolerant		Nice light color, lights up the shade. Evergreen.	yes	fern	yes

Scientific name	Common name	Light	Moisture	Bloom time	Comments	Native?	Type	Deer resistant?
Dicentra spp.	bleeding heart	●	Wet tolerant	April	Heart shaped flowers, usually pink or white. Leaves on most varieties disappear in summer. *Dicentra eximia* is native.	some	perennial	yes
Digitalis spp.	foxglove	○ ◑ ●		summer	Flowers on spike.	some	biennial	yes
Dryopteris marginalis	evergreen wood fern	◑ ●				yes	fern	yes
Dryopteris x australis	Dixie wood fern	●			Tall, upright fronds.	yes	fern	yes
Echinacea purpurea	cone flower	○ ◑	Drought tolerant	July		yes	perennial	may nibble
Eupatorium dubium	Joe-Pye weed	○ ◑	Wet tolerant	Aug - Sept	Bees and butterflies love it. Long lasting blooms.	yes	perennial	yes
Euphorbia spp.	shrubby spurges	varies		spring	Evergreen. Odd green flowers.	some	perennial	some
Eurybia divaricata	white wood aster	◑		Sept - Oct		yes	perennial	yes
Forsythia spp.	forsythia	○ ◑		March	Profuse yellow flowers.	no	shrub	yes
Fothergilla spp.	fothergilla, witch alder	○ ◑		spring		yes		
Galanthus nivalis	snowdrop	◑ ●		March	The first sign of spring.	no	bulbs	yes

Scientific name	Common name	Light	Moisture	Bloom time	Comments	Native?	Type	Deer resistant?
Gardenia jasminoides 'Summer Snow'	Summer Snow gardenia	○		May - June	Evergreen. New gardenia that is hardy here. Heavenly smell.	no	shrub	
Geranium maculatum	spotted geranium, spotted cranesbill	○ ◐		June	Scanty mound with small pink flowers.	yes	perennial	some
Hamamelis spp.	witch hazel	○ ◐ ●		Nov or spring	Yellow flowers that bloom in late fall or late winter, depending on the species.	yes	shrub	?
Helleborus orientali	lenten rose	○ ◐ ●		Feb - March	Evergreen. Down pointing flowers. Search for varieties that point up.	no	perennial	yes
Hemerocallis spp.	daylily	○ ◐ ●	Drought and wet tolerant	summer	More sun means more blooms. Avoid H. fulva and H. lilioasphodelus, which are an invasive threat in Virginia.	no	perennial	no
Heuchera villosa	coral bells, maple-leaved alumroot	○ ◐		late summer	Watch out for new cultivars: they tend to die.	yes	perennial	yes
Heucherella spp.	heucherella	◐ ●		summer	Cross between Heuchera and Tiarella.	no	perennial	?
Hexastylus spp.	evergreen ginger	●		spring	ground-cover	yes	perennial	yes
Hibiscus spp.	hardy hibiscus	○		July	Some need wet feet.	some	shrub	some

151

Scientific name	Common name	Light	Moisture	Bloom time	Comments	Native?	Type	Deer resistant?
Hosta spp.	hosta	◐		summer	Many species, different sizes. Avoid afternoon sun.	no	perennial	no
Hydrangea spp.	hydrangea	○ ◐		May–July	Many species, including some nice natives. *H. quercifolia* (oak-leaf hydrangeas) a drought and wet tolerant native that gets quite tall. *H. arborescens* has beautiful big white blooms.	some	shrub	no
Hypericum perforatum	St. John's wort	○ ◐		summer	Huge yellow pompon flowers. Honey bees and bumble bees love it.	yes	perennial	yes
Ilex glabra	inkberry	○ ◐ ●	Wet tolerant	late spring		yes	shrub	yes
Ilex opaca	American holly	○ ◐		spring	Evergreen with red berries. Grows very large, so don't plant near walk, driveway or anything else. Must be pruned often to be kept small.	yes	tree	yes

Scientific name	Common name	Light	Moisture	Bloom time	Comments	Native?	Type	Deer resistant?
Ilex verticillata 'Red Sprite'	winterberry holly	○ ◐ ●	Wet tolerant	spring	Vivid red berries stand out after leaves fall off. Needs a male companion to produce berries.	yes	shrub	?
Iris spp.	iris	○ ◐	Drought tolerant	May	Virginia blue flag is wet tolerant. Avoid yellow flag (I. pseudacorus) which is an invasive alien.	some	bulbs	yes
Itea virginica 'Henry's garnet'	Virginia sweetspire	○ ◐	Wet tolerant	early summer	An excellent alternative to the invasive butterfly bush. Butterflies prefer this. Unlike the butterfly bush, flowers bloom on old wood.	yes	shrub	no
Jeffersonia diphylla	twinleaf	●	Drought tolerant		ground-cover with curious seed pods.	yes	perennial	?
Juniperus squamata 'Blue Star'	blue star juniper	○	Drought tolerant		Beautiful blue green color, compact. Great for rock gardens. Can tolerate some shade.	no	shrub	?
Kalmia latifolia	mountain laurel	○ ◐ ●		May		yes	shrub	no

153

Scientific name	Common name	Light	Moisture	Bloom time	Comments	Native?	Type	Deer resistant?
Kniphofi	red hot poker	○ ◑	Drought tolerant	June	Spiky succulent leaves with dramatic orange/red flowers on a spike.	no	perennial	yes
Lavendula angustifolia	lavender	○ ◑		June	Spiky green leaves, flower spikes of subtle purple flowers. Pruning may kill it. Needs well drained soil.	no	shrub	yes
Leucanthemum x superbum	Shasta daisy	○ ◑		July	Standard white daisy, very easy.	no	perennial	no
Liatris spicata	gayfeather, dense blazing star, prairie gay feather	○ ◑	Wet tolerant	summer	Purple spikes.	yes	perennial	yes
Ligularia spp.	leopard plant	○ ◑	Wet tolerant	summer	Needs wet feet.	no	perennial	yes
Lilium spp.	oriental lilies	○		June - July	Many species.	no	perennial	no
Lindera benzoin	spicebush	○ ◑ ●	Wet tolerant	early spring	Needs sun to make many berries.	yes	shrub	yes
Liriope muscari	liriope	●		summer	Grass-like leaves, subtle flowers. Shear back in late winter. Tough as nails. Avoid *Liriope spicata*, which is invasive.	no	perennial	yes

Reliable perennials list

Scientific name	Common name	Light	Moisture	Bloom time	Comments	Native?	Type	Deer resistant?
Lobelia cardinalis	ardinal flower	○ ◐	Wet tolerant	late summer	Red flowers. Self-sows. Needs wet feet.	yes	perennial	?
Lychnis coronaria	rose campion	○	Drought tolerant	June	Silvery fuzzy leaves, vivid red/pink flowers. Original plant often will not reappear but self-seeds. Has potential to become invasive.	no	biennial	yes
Magnolia grandiflora	southern magnolia, bull bay	○ ◐ ●		June	Evergreen tree with showy flowers and leaves that lend a tropical look. The limbs may break under heavy snow, but remaining branches thrive.	yes	tree	yes
Magnolia x soulangeana	saucer magnolia	○ ◐		April	Big tree, spectacular pink flowers.	no	tree	no
Matteuccia struthiopteris	ostrich fern	◐ ●	Wet tolerant		Large (3 to 5 feet tall)	yes	fern	yes
Mertensia virginica	Virginia bluebells	◐	Wet tolerant	April	Small blue flowers. Thrives in river bottoms that flood.	yes		yes
Monarda didyma	bee balm	○ ◐	Wet tolerant	summer	Interesting red flowers. Tall. Hummingbirds love it.	yes	perennial	yes

Scientific name	Common name	Light	Moisture	Bloom time	Comments	Native?	Type	Deer resistant?
Monarda fistulosa	wild bergamot, bee balm	○ ◐	Drought tolerant	summer	Purplish flowers.	yes	perennial	yes
Muhlenbergia capillaris	muhly grass	○			Show-stopping late season color. Billowy pink flowers.	yes	grass	yes
Narcissus spp.	daffodil, narcissus	◐ ●		March	Let leaves die naturally before trimming.	no	bulbs	yes
Nepeta spp.	catmint	○		June	Green mound with subtle blue flowers. Use a hoop stake to keep the nice round mound shape.	no	perennial	yes
Oenothera fruticosa	sundrops	○	Drought tolerant	May		yes	perennial	yes
Onoclea sensibilis	sensitive fern	○ ◐ ●	Wet tolerant			yes	fern	yes
Osmunda cinnamomea	cinnamon fern	○ ◐ ●	Drought and wet tolerant			yes	fern	yes
Pachysandra procumbens	native pachysandra	◐ ●	Drought tolerant	spring	The native alternative to the more popular but invasive Japanese version. Takes much longer to spread.	yes	perennial	yes

Scientific name	Common name	Light	Moisture	Bloom time	Comments	Native?	Type	Deer resistant?
Paeonia spp.	peony	○ ◐		May-June	Dramatic pink or red flowers, like giant roses. Use a wire cage to hold them up. Many species.	no	perennial	yes
Panicum virgatum	switchgrass	○ ◐	Drought and wet tolerant		Ornamental grass. Stays upright even in storms. 'Northwind' is bluish; 'Shenandoah' turns red in the fall.	yes	grass	yes
Papaver orientale	oriental poppy	○		late spring	Staking helps.	no	shrub	yes
Perovskia atriplicifolia	Russian sage	○	Drought tolerant	summer	Silvery leaves with purple flowers. Give it lots of room: gets misshapen if pruned.	no	perennial	yes
Phlox divaricata	woodland phlox	◐	Drought and wet tolerant	April	Lovely light blue flowers.	yes	perennial	?
Phlox paniculata	summer phlox	○ ◐ ●	Drought and wet tolerant	summer	Tall and beautiful. White 'David' variety very popular.	yes	perennial	?
Phlox stolonifera	creeping phlox	◐ ●	Drought tolerant	spring	Forms a dense, semi-evergreen carpet. Can make a great groundcover with a spectacular bloom in the spring.	yes	perennial	?

Scientific name	Common name	Light	Moisture	Bloom time	Comments	Native?	Type	Deer resistant?
Phlox subulata	moss phlox	○	Drought tolerant	spring	Very similar to phlox stolonifera, only truly evergreen and likes sun.	yes	perennial	?
Platycodon grandiflorus	balloon flower	○ ◐		July	Best staked.	no	perennial	no
Podophyllum peltatum	Mayapple	◐ ●	Drought tolerant	spring	Ground-cover for areas with a lot of space.	yes	perennial	yes
Polemonium reptans	Jacob's ladder	●	Drought and wet tolerant		Fronds of leaves with subtle flowers; grown for the foliage.	yes	perennial	yes
Polygonatum falcatum 'Variegatum'	Solomon seal (variegated) (native)	◐ ●	Drought and wet tolerant		Lights up the shade, great in mass plantings. Good substitute for hosta.	yes	perennial	?
Polystichum acrostichoides	Christmas fern	◐ ●	Drought tolerant			yes	fern	yes
Porteranthus spp.	Indian-physic	○ ◐	Drought tolerant	summer		yes	perennial	?
Potentilla simplex	cinquefoil, five fingers, sunkfield, synkefoyle	○ ◐	Drought tolerant		These vines look like mini wild strawberries and make an excellent groundcover, spreading like mad and tolerant of being walked on.	yes	perennial	yes
Pulmonaria spp.	lungwort	◐ ●		spring	Interesting leaves.	no	perennial	yes

Scientific name	Common name	Light	Moisture	Bloom time	Comments	Native?	Type	Deer resistant?
Pycnanthemum muticum	clustered mountain mint	○◐	Drought tolerant		Spreads very aggressively. Really nice pale green flowers that last a long time.	yes	perennial	yes
Pycnanthemum virginianum	Virginia mountain mint	○◐	Drought tolerant		Spreads very aggressively	yes	perennial	yes
Rhododendron spp.	azalea	○◐		April-May	Azaleas are a type of rhododendron. Deer trim away all the flower buds.	some	shrub	no
Rhododendron spp.	evergreen rhododendron species	○◐●		May	Deer usually leave them alone.	some	shrub	?
Rhus 'Gro-low'	'Gro-low' sumac	○◐	Drought tolerant	summer	Low shrub good for erosion control. Great fall color.	yes	shrub	yes
Rudbeckia hirta	black-eyed Susan	○◐	Drought and wet tolerant	July - Sept	Self-seeds.	yes	perennial	yes
Sanguinaria canadensis	bloodroot	◐●	Drought tolerant	spring	Ground-cover	yes	perennial	?
Sarcococca hookeriana var. humilis	sweetbox	◐●		March	Low growing evergreen shrub. Can work as a ground-cover.	no	shrub	yes
Schizachyrium scoparium	little bluestem	○			Larval host for butterflies	yes	grass	yes

Reliable perennials list

Scientific name	Common name	Light	Moisture	Bloom time	Comments	Native?	Type	Deer resistant?
Scilla spp.	squill	●		March	Tiny dark blue flowers for a blue carpet under trees.	no	bulb	yes
Sedum telephium 'Autumn Joy'	sedum 'Autumn Joy'	○	Drought tolerant	Aug - Sept	Succulent. Interesting seed heads in fall	no	perennial	?
Sedum ternatum	woodland stonecrop	○ ◐ ●	Drought tolerant		Succulent. The only shade tolerant sedum; makes a satisfactory ground-cover for dry shade.	yes	perennial	?
Smilacina racemosa	false Solomon's seal, false spiknard, treacleberry	◐ ●		spring	Works as a ground-cover.	yes	perennial	yes
Solidago spp.	goldenrod	○	Drought tolerant		Some are wet tolerant.	yes	perennial	yes
Sorghastrum nutans	Indian grass	○			Tall clump grass, beautiful seed heads.	yes	grass	yes
Spigelia marilandica	Indian pink	◐ ●		May	Red flowers	yes	perennial	no
Stachys byzantina	lamb's ears	○ ◐	Drought tolerant	June	Soft, fuzzy slivery leaves. Grown for its foliage. Spreads quickly. Lower leaves turn brown and form an unattractive mat.	no	perennial	yes
Stylophorum diphyllum	celandine poppy	◐ ●		spring		yes	perennial	yes

Scientific name	Common name	Light	Moisture	Bloom time	Comments	Native?	Type	Deer resistant?
Styrax americanus	American snowbell	◐ ●		spring		yes	tree	yes
Syringa spp.	lilac	○		April	Purple, heavenly smelling flowers.	no	shrub	some
Thelypteris noveboracensis	New York fern	◐ ●	Drought tolerant		Spreads easily.	yes	fern	yes
Tiarella cordifolia	foam flower	●		April	Short broad leaves with spikes of white flowers.	yes	perennial	yes
Trachelospermum jasminoides	Confederate jasmine	○ ◐			Lovely smell.	no	vine	
Tradescantia virginiana	spider wort, Virginia spider wort	○ ◐ ●	Wet tolerant	May-June	Grass-like leaves with clusters of purple flowers. Only blooms in the morning.	yes	perennial	yes
Tricyrtis spp.	toad lily	○ ◐		summer		no	perennial	yes
Trillium spp.	trillium	◐ ●		spring	Slowly forms clumps. Takes seven years to bloom.	yes	perennial	?
Uvularia spp.	merrybells, bellwort	○ ◐		spring	Ground-cover	yes	perennial	?
Vaccinium spp.	blueberry	○	Wet tolerant		Plant more than one variety to get plentiful fruit.	yes	shrub	no
Vernonia noveboracensis	New York ironweed	○	Drought and wet tolerant	Sept	Nice purple flowers.	yes	perennial	yes

Reliable perennials list

Scientific name	Common name	Light	Moisture	Bloom time	Comments	Native?	Type	Deer resistant?
Viburnum acerifolium	mapleleaf viburnum	◐		late spring		yes	shrub	yes
Viburnum dentatum	arrowwood viburnum	◐	Wet tolerant	late spring	Yellow flowers in early spring, lemony fragrance. More than one needed to make berries.	yes	shrub	yes
Viburnum prunifolium	blackhaw, sweet haw, stag bush	◐		early spring		yes	shrub	yes
Yucca filamentosa	yucca	◐	Drought tolerant		Bold ever-green. Once established, only herbicide will remove it.	yes	perennial	yes
Zenobia pul-verulenta 'Woodlander's Blue'	dusty zenobia	◐		spring	Bluish leaves turn vivid red in fall and keep their leaves all winter.	yes	shrub	?

162

Reliable annuals for our climate

Annuals generally bloom all summer and add a lot of color to the garden. Most annuals are perennial somewhere warmer: very few plants in their native habitat die completely every year and have to start over from seed. So, pretty much by definition, annuals are not native plants. Even Indian blankets *(Gaillardia pulchella),* which are native to Virginia, are perennial further south.

Some annuals are relatively deer resistant. A few are drought tolerant but will still need regular watering to become established. Most will do better in rich, amended soil.

Abbreviations:
- ○ Full Sun
- ◖ Part Sun/Shade
- ● Shade
- spp. Species

Reliable annuals list

Scientific name	Common name	Light	Moisture	Native?	Comment	Deer resistant?
Ageratum spp.	ageratum	○ ◑		no		yes
Antirrhinum spp.	snapdragon	○ ◑		no	Prefer cool weather.	yes
Begonia spp.	begonia	○ ◑ ●		no	You can dig them up in the fall, keep them inside, and plant them again in the spring.	?
Calendula spp.	pot marigold	○ ◑	Drought tolerant	no		yes
Catharanthus roseus	annual vinca	○		no	Great container plant. Self-seeds.	yes
Centaurea cineraria	dusty miller	○ ◑	Drought tolerant	no	Grown for silvery foliage.	yes
Cleome hassleriana	spider flower	○	Drought tolerant	no	Self-seeds for years. Nice tall plant to fill in the gaps.	yes
Cosmos bipinnatus	garden cosmos, Mexican aster	○	Drought tolerant	no	Self-seeds. Often planted in median strips on highways. Very tall.	?
Dahlia spp.	dahlia	○		no	If you lift the corns in the fall after the first frost and store them, you can plant them again the next year. The leaves must be killed by frost before you dig them, or you can just let them die and buy more the next year.	no
Fuschia spp.	fuschia	◑ ●		no	Mostly used in hanging baskets. Needs plenty of fertilizer.	no
Gaillardia pulchella	Indian blanket	○	Drought tolerant	yes	Self-seeds. There are other blanket-flowers that are native to the USA; this one is native to Virginia itself.	no
Gladiolus spp.	gladiolus	○		no	Plant from tuber. Occasionally comes up again another year. Lift the tuber in fall if you want to be sure.	yes

164

Scientific name	Common name	Light	Moisture	Native?	Comment	Deer re-sistant?
Gomphrena spp.	globe amaranth	○	Drought tolerant	no		yes
Helichrysum monstrosum	strawflower	○	Drought tolerant	no	Good dried flowers.	yes
Heliotropium spp.	heliotrope	○ ◑	Drought tolerant	no		yes
Impatiens walleriana	impatiens, bizzy Lizzy	◑ ●		no	Very easy to grow. The more sun it gets, the more water it needs.	no
Lantana camara	lantana	○	Drought tolerant	no	Cut back to get a second bloom.	yes
Lobularia maritima	sweet alyssum	○		no		yes
Mandevilla spp.	mandevilla	○		no	Beautiful flowering vine. Don't bother trying to winter it inside: it will not make it. Many different species.	some
Nicotiana spp.	flowering tobacco	○ ◑	Drought tolerant	no		yes
Pelargonium spp.	geranium	○	Drought and wet tolerant	no	You can dig them up in the fall, keep them inside, and plant them again in the spring.	?
Petunia spp.	petunia	○ ◑	Drought tolerant	no	Ruthlessly pinch them back regularly-- they will reward you with many more blooms.	?
Portulaca grandiflora	portulaca, moss rose	○	Drought tolerant	no		no
Solenostemon spp.	coleus	◑ ●		no	Great foliage plants. Do beautifully in containers if you get the short variety.	no
Tagetes spp.	marigold, common mar-igold	○ ◑	Drought tolerant	no	*Tagetes patula* (French marigolds) are more likely to be deer resistant and useful as companion plants to repel harmful insects.	?
Tithonia rotundifolia	Mexican sunflower	○		no	Tall and ungainly, but much longer blooming than regular sunflowers. Butterflies and hummingbirds love it.	yes

Scientific name	Common name	Light	Moisture	Native?	Comment	Deer re-sistant?
Tropaeolum majus	nasturtium	○	Drought tolerant	no	Best planted from seed.	yes
Viola × wittrockiana	pansy	◑		no	Planted in the fall, they keep their flowers all winter then start to grow in early spring. They disappear when the weather gets hot.	no
Zinnia spp.	zinnia	○	Drought tolerant	no		yes

Fuschia

Four season gardening

There are numerous strategies to add fall and winter interest to your garden. Here are a few suggestions.

Interesting flower seed heads
> *Sedum telephium 'Autumn Joy'* Three feet tall

Brilliant red fall foliage
> *Itea virginica 'Henry's garnet'* (Virginia sweetspire) A good substitute for the invasive *Euonymus alatus* (burning bush)
> *Vaccinium* (blueberries) Often have vivid fall colors and/or red twigs

Peeling bark
> birch trees
> sycamore trees

Colored bark
> *Cornus sericea* (redtwig dogwood)
> *Cornus sericea* 'Flaviramea' (yellow twig dogwood)
> *Acer palmatum* 'Sango Kaku' (coral bark Japanese maple) Has red twigs
> *Acer negundo* 'Winter Lightning' (box elder maple) Has yellow twigs

Interesting twisted limbs
> *Corylus avellana* 'Contorta' (Henry Lauder's walking stick)
> *Acer palmatum* (Japanese maples)

Bright colored berries
> *Viburnum dentatum* and other viburnums
> Winterberry holly (such as *Ilex verticillata* 'Red Sprite')
> American beautyberry (*Callicarpa americana*) Purple berries

Evergreens
> Low spreading yews
> Lots of other things including some types of azaleas – check out the labels!

Evergreen ground covers
> *Sarcococca hookeriana var. humilis* (sweetbox) Blooms in early March
> *Jasminum nudilflorum* (winter jasmine) Blooms in February!

Evergreen perennials
> Hellebores Totally deer proof, bloom in February. Try to find a variety with upward pointing flowers

Unusual bloom times
> Depending on the variety, *Hamamelis* (witch hazels) bloom after their leaves fall off in November, or February, but beware! These latter need lots of winter sun to bloom.
> Camellias bloom either around Thanksgiving or very early spring.

Ornamental grasses

Pansies
> Pansies planted in the fall will often survive even through blizzards.

Ornamental cabbage/kale
> Very pretty and very hardy in this zone

Cheat
> Pretty arbors, pots, birdbaths, *etc.,* will keep their looks yea round.

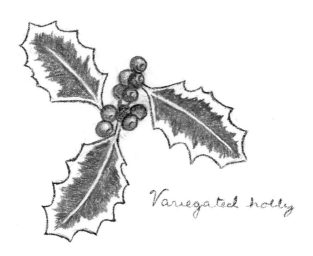

Variegated holly

Rain gardens

Building a rain garden is a very significant way to demonstrate that we understand what a tremendous impact we have had on our local environment. We have removed acres and acres of trees (which allow rain water to percolate slowly into the ground) and replaced them with acres and acres of buildings, lawn, and asphalt, which causes rain water to drain rapidly into nearby streams. Fairfax County tries to mitigate this by creating sumps along new highways such as the Fairfax County Parkway. In addition to conveying pollutants, run-off rapidly erodes stream banks, destroying the shade trees that drop their leaves into the water. The warmer water becomes uninhabitable to the small organisms that form the basis for the food chain, as they cannot tolerate the higher temperature and need the dead leaves for food. In addition, a portion of the chemicals we apply to our lawn and garden drain off the property and eventually wind up in the Chesapeake Bay. Rain gardens are an indication that the resident is aware of the destruction we are inadvertently causing to our environment and is attempting to do something about it.

Rain gardens attempt to intercept some portion of the water draining off the property into a shallow "basin" that has been specifically prepared with very porous soil to enable the water to percolate into the soil within the basin. That soil can be made porous by adding lots of peat moss and humus material but must remain a few inches below the rim of the basin so that rain water collects within. If the rain garden is placed and prepared properly, plants such as ferns will thrive.

A rain garden is most practical if there is a spot in the yard that either has or could use a garden. Instead of raising the soil so that excess rain runs off, as one would usually do when installing a garden, the soil is made very porous so that large amounts of water soak into the soil.

One technique is to construct a French drain. The cost of the materials is about $25. Dig a one foot deep trench across the low point of your property, and then connect it with another trench to your house. Lay in the trench a plastic pipe with holes, and connect it to the downspout. Cover with pebbles under a thin layer of top soil. Build up a six inch berm on the downhill side of the horizontal trench to catch whatever rain water might overflow from the French drain.

A rototiller makes constructing a rain garden easier but is certainly not essential. The rototiller would be used to loosen the ground up-hill of the berm in order to create a slightly larger basin in front of the berm.

Some plants are well adapted to soil that gets soggy but which can also dry out completely at times. Examples include Virginia sweetspire (*Itea virginica*), black-eyed Susan (*Rudbeckia hirta*), winterberry holly (*Ilex verticillata 'Red Sprite'*), arrowwood viburnum (*Viburnum dentatum*), willows *(Salix)*, switchgrass *(Panicum virgatum)*, cardinal flower (*Lobelia cardinalis*), butterfly weed (*Asclepias tuberosa*), redtwig dogwood (*Cornus sericea*) and sweet pepperbush (*Clethra anilfolia*).

There are lots of details about appropriate plants as well as construction techniques available on the web.

Rain barrels are another way to prevent some of the water from running off your property. A rain barrel could connect to a soaker hose with the cock continuously open. This way your downspout water collects in the barrel and is redistributed over your garden rather than turning into run-off. You can also connect more than one rain barrel in a series in order to increase the capacity.

If you are paving your driveway, consider using permeable paving techniques instead of solid pavement. There are a variety of options available, including loose gravel, porous concrete and asphalt, and open-jointed blocks which leave space between the individual units.

Local garden centers

We are blessed in this region by a large number and variety of garden centers, everything from small seasonal affairs to high end nurseries with every plant, tool and accessory you could ever wish for. We list here a few that our sources happened to mention as their favorites. My deepest apologies for the many left out simply because there are too many for me to have heard of them all. We will be happy to include them in a future edition!

In addition to the dedicated garden centers, many serious gardeners also mentioned being very satisfied with Lowe's and Home Depot. Although they have considerably less variety, their plants, bagged mulch and soil are less expensive than elsewhere, and of course they carry very solid lines of tools, pots and other accessories. Some downsides to buying perennials, shrubs and trees at a big box store is that expert helps is often hard to find, and the selection dwindles after spring. (It is better to plant in the fall when you can.)

Local garden centers list

Betty's Azalea Ranch 12507 Lee Highway, Fairfax, VA 22030
703-830-8687
- Tools, supplies, accessories? Yes
- Special orders? Yes
- Deliver and install? Yes
- Take back and reuse pots? Some
- Plant guarantees? Yes
- Landscaping design or consultation? Yes
- Equipment rentals? Core aerators and compost spreaders
- When open: Year round.

Comments: Knowledgeable advice.

Blue Mount Nursery 20052 Lexington Drive, Ashburn, VA 20147
703-729-6600
- Tools, supplies, accessories? Yes
- Special orders? Yes
- Deliver and install? Yes
- Take back and reuse pots? Yes
- Plant guarantees? Yes
- Landscaping design or consultation? Yes
- Equipment rentals? No

Burke Nursery 9401 Burke Road, Burke, VA 22015 703-323-1188
- Tools, supplies, accessories? Yes
- Special orders? Yes
- Deliver and install? Yes
- Take back and reuse pots? No
- Plant guarantees? 1 year if they plant, 6 months if you plant
- Landscaping design or consultation? Yes
- Equipment rentals? Occasionally has a rototiller or sod roller available
- When open: Year round.

Comments: Good variety. Sells vegetables in 3 packs and 6 packs, which are more economical if you are planting a large garden. In the fall they have a Pumpkin Playground.

Campbell & Ferrara Outdoor Living 6651 Little River Turnpike, Alexandria, VA 22312 703-354-6724
- Tools, supplies, accessories? Some
- Special orders? Yes
- Deliver and install? Yes
- Take back and reuse pots? No
- Plant guarantees? Trees and shrubs only. 1 year if they plant and 6 months if you plant
- Landscaping design or consultation? Yes
- Equipment rentals? Occasionally has a rototiller or sod roller available
- When open: Year round.

Comments: Nice variety, wonderful roses, good landscaping. Playground. Free seminars on Saturdays.

Cox Farms 15621 Braddock Road, Centreville, VA 20120   703-830-4121
- Tools, supplies, accessories? Limited
- Special orders? Yes
- Deliver and install? No
- Take back and reuse pots? Yes
- Plant guarantees? Yes
- Landscaping design or consultation? No
- Equipment rentals? No
- When open: Opens in March

Comments: Beautiful, healthy plants, good variety.

DeBaggio's Herb Farm and Nursery 43494 Mountain View Drive, Chantilly, VA 703-327-6976
- Open: Spring to July 1

Green Springs Gardens 603 Green Spring Road Alexandria, VA 22312 703-642-5173
- Tools, supplies, accessories? Very limited
- Special orders? No
- Deliver and install? No
- Take back and reuse pots? No
- Plant guarantees? No
- Landscaping design or consultation? No

- Equipment rentals? No
- When open: April to October

Comments: A small but choice collection of plants propagated at Green Springs Gardens. Native plants.

Heather Hill 8111 Ox Road, Fairfax Station, VA 703-690-6060
- Tools, supplies, accessories? No
- Special orders? Sometimes
- Deliver and install? No
- Take back and reuse pots? Yes
- Plant guarantees? Yes
- Landscaping design or consultation? Yes
- Equipment rentals? No
- When open: Open April 1- November 1

Comments: Hard to find and unusual perennials and annuals. Grow some of their own on site. Knowledgeable staff that have time to talk. Display gardens: ask them about their vole cages! Carries over 50 kinds of hostas and 50 kinds of herbs.

Holly, Woods and Vines 8453 Richmond Highway, Alexandria, VA 22309 703-799-1607
- Tools, supplies, accessories? Yes
- Special orders? Sometimes
- Deliver and install? Yes
- Take back and reuse pots? No
- Plant guarantees? 6 months if you plant, 1 year if they do.
- Landscaping design or consultation? Yes
- Equipment rentals? No
- When open: Year round

Comments: Good selection.

Meadows Farms Nurseries 24 locations
- Tools, supplies, accessories? Yes
- Special orders? Yes
- Deliver and install? Yes
- Take back and reuse pots? Yes
- Plant guarantees? 6 months
- Landscaping design or consultation? Yes

- Equipment rentals? No
- When open: March 1 - December 24

Comments: Good prices.

Merrifield Garden Center 3 locations:

Merrifield: 8132 Lee Highway, Merrifield, VA 22116   703-560-6222

Fair Oaks: 12101 Lee Highway, Fairfax, VA 22030 703-968-9600

Gainesville: 6895 Wellington Rd, Gainesville, VA 20156 703-368-1919

- Tools, supplies, accessories? Yes
- Special orders? Yes
- Deliver and install? Yes
- Take back and reuse pots? No
- Plant guarantees? Trees and shrubs
- Landscaping design or consultation? Yes. Also handyman service.
- Equipment rentals? Sod roller, ball cart, compost spreaders
- When open: Year round

Comments: Excellent centers, with all kinds of healthy plants including houseplants. Extremely knowledgeable staff. All kinds of garden tools and ornaments. Free seminars on Saturdays. The Gainesville center is the Mall of America of garden centers! Huge inventory of plants and everything else. Even has a cafe, dog park and wine shop.

Nalls Produce 7310 Beulah Street, Franconia, VA 22315
703-971-4068

- Tools, supplies, accessories? minimal
- Special orders? Yes
- Deliver and install? Yes
- Take back and reuse pots? No
- Plant guarantees? Trees and shrubs
- Landscaping design or consultation? Yes
- Equipment rentals? No
- When open: Spring to Thanksgiving

Comments: Nice selection.

Nature by Design 300 Calvert Avenue, Alexandria, VA 22301
703-683-4769
- Tools, supplies, accessories? No
- Special orders? Yes, depending
- Deliver and install? Yes
- Take back and reuse pots? Yes
- Plant guarantees? 1 year
- Landscaping design or consultation?   Yes
- Equipment rentals? No
- When open: Regular retail hours in season. Open by appointment on-ly during the holidays and into mid-January.

Comments: All native plants.

Sam's Farm 7125 Leesburg Pike Falls, Church VA 22043 703-534-5292
- Tools, supplies, accessories? Yes
- Special orders? Yes, depending
- Deliver and install? Delivery but not installation
- Take back and reuse pots? Yes
- Plant guarantees? No
- Landscaping design or consultation? No
- Equipment rentals? No
- When open: Late March through Christmas

Comments: Lots of garden statues.

Silverbrook Nursery and Landscaping 8408 Monacan Road, Lorton, VA
22079 703-690-1231
- Tools, supplies, accessories? some
- Special orders? Yes, depending
- Deliver and install? Yes
- Take back and reuse pots? No
- Plant guarantees? Only if they plant it
- Landscaping design or consultation? Yes
- Equipment rentals? No
- When open: Year round

Comments: Park-like grounds with playground, demonstration gardens. Par-ticularly charming accessories for sale such as decorated trellises and other ornaments.

Treefrog Nursery 11100 Georgetown Pike, Great Falls, VA 22066
703-467-9800
- Tools, supplies, accessories? Yes
- Special orders? sometimes
- Deliver and install? Yes
- Take back and reuse pots? No
- Plant guarantees?
- Landscaping design or consultation? Yes
- Equipment rentals? No
- When open: Spring until Thanksgiving

Comments: Specializes in container gardening, native plants.

Wolf Trap Nursery 9439 Leesburg Pike Vienna, VA 22182   703-759-4244
- Tools, supplies, accessories? Yes
- Special orders? Yes
- Deliver and install? Yes
- Take back and reuse pots? No
- Plant guarantees? 1 year 100% if they plant tree or shrub, 50% if you plant it
- Landscaping design or consultation? Yes
- Equipment rentals? No
- When open: Year round

Comments: Big collection of bonsais and the tools needed for planting them; bonsai workshops

Public gardens

Northern Virginia

Ben Lomond Historic Site and Old Rose Garden 10311 Sudley Manor Drive, Manassas, VA
> Collection of antique roses, most dating from the 19th century or earlier. Manor house used as Civil War hospital.

Bon Air Park and Rose Garden   850 North Lexington Street, Arlington, VA 703-358-4747
> Horticultural gardens: Azalea/Camellia Garden, Ornamental Tree Garden, Sun Garden, Shade Garden, Wildflower Area, Memorial Rose Garden.

Bull Run Regional Park 7700 Bull Run Drive, Centreville, VA 703-631-0550
> Spectacular drifts of Virginia blue bells bloom in mid to late April.

Carlyle House 121 N. Fairfax Street, Alexandria, VA 22314
> Historic garden in Old Town Alexandria.

Green Spring Gardens 603 Green Spring Road, Alexandria, VA 22312 703-642-5173
> Large and beautiful gardens with education center, perennial garden store, succulent room, small bookshop, large library. Master Gardeners course and many short programs. Sign up for

the latter through ParkTakes or by calling Green Springs. Gardens are arranged to be educational, with displays including demonstration townhouse gardens, roses, perennials, native plants, *etc.* Well labeled.

The Native Arboretum, Marie Butler Leven Preserve 1501 Kirby Road, McLean, VA 22101
> An Earth Sangha project. Volunteers needed. Started in 2004 and still a work in progress.

Oatlands Plantation 20850 Oatlands Plantation Lane, Leesburg, VA 20175
> Formal garden, nice winter interest.

River Farm 7931 East Boulevard Drive, Alexandria, VA 22308 703-768-5700
> Nice gardens, mostly labeled, with spectacular meadow of over 100,000 plants leading down to the Potomac. Great place to go if you want to see how a meadow could look.

Rippon Lodge Historic Site 15520 Blackburn Road, Woodbridge, VA 703-499-9812
> Has 42 acres of grounds with old growth trees such as elms. Early 20th century decorative garden. Free access to grounds, small charge for tours of 1747 house.

Winkler Botanical Preserve 5400 Roanoke Avenue, Alexandria, VA 22311
> Pleasant stroll in the woods around a pond with native plantings. Educational center for school groups.

Meadowlark Botanical Gardens 9750 Meadowlark Gardens Court, Vienna, VA 22182
> This 95 acre garden contains both ornamental and conservation collections with extensive native plant displays, a visitor center

and book shop as well as a reception venue. Knowledgeable staff makes for very educational visits. Mostly labeled.

D.C. metro area

Bishop's Garden, Washington National Cathedral, Massachusetts and Wisconsin Ave, NW, Washington, DC 20016-5098
   The Bishops Garden on the grounds of the Washington National Cathedral is wonderful. It is free and open to the public seven days a week. Gardeners are usually working there on Tuesdays and will be happy to answer questions. There is list of the flowering plants available for free in the little Herb Cottage that is near the entrance to the garden. They update the list every two months.

Brookside Gardens Wheaton Regional Park, 1400 Glenallen Ave., Wheaton, MD. 301-946-9071
   Beautiful landscaping, very large garden, well-labeled plants. Free.

Constitution Gardens 900 Ohio Drive, SW, Washington, DC 202-426-6841

Dumbarton Oaks and Gardens R and 31st Streets, NW, Washington, DC
   Beautiful formal gardens. Also good in winter.

Hillwood Mansion and Garden 4155 Linnean Avenue, NW, Washington, DC 202-686-8500
   Specializes in woodland plants, Japanese garden.

Kenilworth Aquatic Gardens 1900 Anacostia Avenue and Douglas Avenue, NE, Washington, DC 202-426-6905
   Roses, wetlands, native plants, and display gardens.

Mount Vernon Estate and Gardens George Washington Parkway, Mount Vernon, VA
> Historical garden.

Old Stone House Garden Old Stone House, 3501 M St., NW, Washington, DC

Tudor Place Historic House and Gardens 1644 31st Street, NW, Washington, DC
> Formal Gardens. South lawn in the manner of an 18th century English park.

U.S. Botanic Garden 245 First St., SW Washington, DC 202-225-8333
> Right next to the Capitol. Great place to get your gardening fix in the winter, as it is entirely enclosed.

U.S. National Arboretum 501 New York Avenue, NE, Washington, DC 202-245-2726
> Great place to bicycle during azalea season. Bonsai, display gardens. Herb, native plant, orchid, perennial, and rose gardens. Conservatory and arboretum.

Day trips

Chanticleer 786 Church Road Wayne, PA 19087-4713 610-687-4163
> Relatively new, this is probably the horticultural high mark in the USA today, if not the world! Imaginative and full of variety.

Longwood Gardens 1001 Longwood Rd, Kennett Square, PA 19348 610-318-1000
> Huge. Amazing gift store. Fountain displays, concerts, fireworks, organ.

Nemours Mansion and Gardens Route 141 (Powder Mill Drive) and Alapocas Road, Wilmington, Delaware 19803

State Arboretum of Virginia Boyce, VA (near Winchester)
Nice herb garden, well labeled. Largest collection of boxwood varieties in North America. Collections of conifers, linden, stewartia, buckeye, maples, hollies, crabapples, quince, magnolia, birches, elms, chestnuts, oaks, azaleas, irises, daylilies, boxwoods, viburnum, *Vitex*, lilacs, catalpa, ashes, *Halesia*, *Styrax*.

Wintherthur 5105 Kennett Pike, Wilmington, DE 19807
Big on mass plantings. Large, dramatic displays such as witch hazels.

Plant sales and garden shows

February

- *Capital Home and Garden* Show   www.capitalhomeshow.com
  Chantilly-Dulles Expo Center

- *Washington Gardener Magazine annual seed exchange*

March

- *Garden Club of Virginia Daffodil* Show   www.gcvirginia.org

- *Philadelphia International Flower Show*
  Huge and amazing. Proof that spring will really come.

- *Washington Home & Garden Show*
  www.washingtonhomeandgardenshow.com
  Washington Convention Center

April

- *American Horticultural Society*   www.ahs.org
  Members can go in the evening before a sale. Good prices,
  good sized plants.

- *Friends of the National Arboretum Garden Fair and Plant Sale*
  www.fona.org
  Includes children's activities and music. Plant sale and fair in
  April, bonsai in May.

- *Huntley Meadows Eco-Savvy Expo* 703-68-2525
  Native plant sale by Nature by Design. Bee boxes, rain barrels,
  native seed mixes and how-to presentation.

- *Leesburg Flower and Garden Festival* www.idalee.org

- *Long Branch Nature Center*
  Arlington. Native plants. Most plants propagated on site.

- *Northern Virginia Soil and Water Conservation District Annual Seedling Sale*
  www.fairfaxcounty.gov/nvswcd/seedlingsale.htm
  The district's annual seedling sale makes low cost native shrub
  and tree seedlings available to Northern Virginia residents.
  Seedling packages go on sale each year in January and are
  available for pickup in mid-April.

- *Park Fairfax Native Plant Sale*
  www.parkfairfaxnativeplantsale.org
  Last Saturday in April and last Saturday in September. Alexandria. Various native plant nurseries from five states set up shop
  for the day.

- *Rust Nature Sanctuary*
  Leesburg

May

- *Ayr Hill Garden Club plant sale*
  Vienna

- *Garden Club of Waynewood tour and sale*
  www.waynewoodgardenclub.com
  May tour; July 4 sale.

- *Great Falls Garden Club* www.gfgardenclub.org
  Annual sale and biennial flower show.

- *Green Springs Garden*
  2nd Saturday of May and 3rd Saturday of September
  About 40 vendors in the spring and 20 in the fall. Great sale
  though crowded.

- *Prince William Wildflower Society Plant Sale*, Virginia Native
  Plant Society
  Saturday before Mother's Day .

- *State Arboretum of Virginia - Garden Fair and Arbor Fest*
  http://blandy.virginia.edu
  Mother's Day weekend and October.

- *U.S. National Arboretum* www.fona.org
  Plant sale and fair in April, bonsai in May.

- *Washington National Cathedral* www.nationalcathedral.org
  Plant sales, floral and horticultural displays, boutique booths,
  tasty foods, music and entertainment, plus fun activities for
  children, including rides on the antique carousel.

June

- *Garden Club of Virginia Lily Show*   www.gcvirginia.org

July

- *Garden Club of Waynewood tour and sale*
  www.waynewoodgardenclub.com
  May tour; July 4 sale.

September

- *Green Springs Garden*
  2nd Saturday of May and 3rd Saturday of September
  About 40 vendors in the spring and 20 in the fall. Great sale
  though crowded.

- *Park Fairfax Native Plant Sale*
  www.parkfairfaxnativeplantsale.org
  Last Saturday in April and last Saturday in September. Alexandria. Various native plant nurseries from five states set up shop
  for the day.

October

- *Garden Club of Virginia Rose Show*   www.gcvirginia.org

- *Old Dominion Chrysanthemum Society Annual Flower Show
  and Exhibition*   www.odcsmums.org

- *State Arboretum of Virginia - Garden Fair and Arbor Fest*
  http://blandy.virginia.edu
  Mother's Day weekend and October.

Dates unavailable

- *Earth Sangha*   www.earthsangha.org
  Native plants. Spring and fall.

- *Garden Club of Montclair annual sale*

- *Putnum Hill*   www.putnamhillnursery.com
  Open houses.

- *Saunders Brothers*   www.saundersbrothers.com
  Open houses. In Piney River, VA. Sells to Merrifield.

- *Willowbrook Garden Club annual sale*
  www.lrcaonline.org/community_org_garden.html
  Held at the Ilda pool.

Annual garden tours

April

Georgetown House Tour www.georgetownhousetour.com

Historic Garden Week (Events in Fairfax and Alexandria)
www.vagardenweek.org

White House garden tour www.whitehouse.gov

May

Capitol Hill Restoration Society House and Garden Tour
www.chrs.org

*Clifton Community Woman's Club Charity Homes Tour and
Marketplace* http://cliftoncwc.org

Georgetown Garden Tour www.georgetowngardentour.com

*Georgetown Garden Treasures Tour (Dumbarton Oaks and Tudor
Place Historic House and Garden)*

June

Watershed Friendly Home, Garden and Horse Farm Tour
www.fairfaxcounty.gov/nvswcd/gardentour.htm

Visit gardens throughout Fairfax County featuring vegetated roofs, rain barrels, backyard wildlife habitat, composting, native plant species and more.

Green Living Home & Garden Tour (Arlington)
www.arlingtonenvironment.org/gardentour.htm#garden

Mail order companies

Plants

Bluestones Perennials www.bluestoneperennials.com 800-852-5243
Ohio
Lots of low-water plants. Nice search function.

Gilbert H Wild and Son www.gilberthwild.com 417-548-3514
Missouri
Daylilies.

Niche Gardens www.nichegardens.com 919-967-0078
North Carolina
Extensive selection of native plants. Good service.

RareFind Nursery www.rarefindnursery.com 732-833-0618
New Jersey
Their plants are larger than the average mail order company, very healthy, and well packed. Specialty: rhododendrons. Personal service.

Bulbs

Van Engelen Inc. www.vanengelen.com 860-567-8734
Connecticut
Bulbs at incredibly low prices.

Seeds

Baker Creek Heirloom Seeds www.rareseeds.com 417-924-8917
Missouri
All natural, no genetically modified seeds.

High Mowing Organic Seeds www.highmowingseeds.com
802-472-6174
> Vermont
> Wide variety of heirlooms.

Johnny's Selected Seeds www.johnnyseeds.com 877-564-6697
> Maine
> Good quality and selection, inexpensive.

Pinetree Garden Seeds www.superseeds.com 207-926-3400
> Maine
> Seeds at much lower prices.

Seeds of Change www.seedsofchange.com 888-762-7333
> California
> Wide variety of heirlooms.

Stoke's Seeds www.stokeseeds.com 800-396-9238
> Ontario
> Good quality and selection, inexpensive.

Vermont Bean Seed Company www.vermontbean.com 800-349-1071
> Wisconsin
> Sell packets with smaller number of seeds, which is more convenient.

Supplies

Gardener's Supply Company www.gardeners.com 888-833-1412
> Pretty much every kind of supply or accessory you could need.

Learn more about gardening

Gardening magazines

Reading a little bit every month will brighten the off season and gradually turn you into an expert. *Virginia Gardener*, for instance, has a regular column on gardening in our part of the state. *Washington Gardener* is full of good articles; you can also sign up for its e-newsletter or join a discussion list. *Garden Gate* comes out quarterly and has incredibly helpful and practical seasonal tips. They always showcase "Ten top picks" of something - vines, shade annuals, whatever - which makes it possible to digest because the information comes in manageable quantities in the right season. *American Gardener* has somewhat longer articles with extensive resource lists.

Radio

Andre Viette (Fishersville, Virginia) conducts a weekly three-hour call-in radio program, "In the Garden," on Saturdays mornings. In Fredericksburg, WFVA, AM 1230. You can stream it on the web or listen to podcasts.

His son, Mark Viette, conducts a two-hour show, "Easy Gardening," Sundays mornings on WOR Radio Network. He has also produced numerous 60-second gardening videos which can be viewed on You Tube.

Mark McGrath, WTOPs "Friday Yard Warrior," broadcasts short segments on Fridays as well as other times. You can listen to his pieces afterwards at the WTOP web site as well as read a written version.

Jos Roozen and Rick Fowler co-host "Garden Sense" on WMAL 105.7, Saturdays 8:00-9:00 am. Their shows are archived at www.radiogardensense.com.

TV
"Merrifield Garden Advisors" airs on News Channel 8 on Saturdays at 8 am. They also have videos posted on You Tube.

Libraries
The public libraries have many shelves full of gardening books on every topic.

Get help with research
If you need to research horticultural matters (such as to write a gardening book), Green Springs Gardens has an extensive reference library and an incredibly helpful librarian!

Workshops
Many organizations hold workshops and seminars, including Green Springs and Meadowlark Botanical gardens, the Virginia Native Plant Society, and some garden centers. Green Springs Gardens and Huntley Meadows Park classes can be accessed via ParkTakes Online, the web site for the Fairfax County Park Authority.

Go back to school
The Northern Virginia Community College offers a degree in horticulture.

Resources

Books

Bringing Nature Home: How you Can Sustain Wildlife with Native Plants, by Douglas W. Tallamy
Amazing book that will convince you to switch to native plants

Native Plants for Wildlife Habitat and Conservation Landscaping: Chesapeake Bay Watershed. US Fish and Wildlife Service
Invaluable primer of native plants, with full details of growing requirements. Unfortunately out of print, but a pdf is on line, and there is a searchable version on their web site. www.nativeplantcenter.net

Organic Gardening: Your Ultimate Resource for Growing a Great Garden and Keeping Ahead of the Pests - Chemical Free, Barbara Ellis and Fern Marshall Bradley, editors
This really is the ultimate reference book for organic gardening. Everything you need to know, with details about diagnosing problems in hundreds of specific plants.

Plant Invaders of Mid-Atlantic Natural Area, National Park Service, Fish and Wildlife Service
Explains the what, why and how of controlling invasive species. www.nps.gov/plants/alien/pubs/midatlantic

Second Nature: A Gardener's Education, by Michael Pollan

The Virginia Gardener's Companion: An Insider's Guide to Low-Maintenance Gardening in Virginia by Donna Williamson
    Very readable and practical.

Wildflowers: A Guide to Growing and Propagating Native Flowers of North America, by William Cullina
    Beautiful detailed book on which natives to plant and how to succeed.

Government agencies

Diagnostic Lab (Virginia Cooperative Extension)
    Bring a sample of whatever is troubling you to any Fairfax County library and ask the staff to send it to the County Extension office. Your sample will be analyzed at the lab, and a detailed diagnosis with recommendations will be mailed back to you.

Home Turf (Virginia Cooperative Extension)
www.fairfaxmastergardeners.org
    For a fee of $25, Master Gardener volunteers come to your property to assess and measure your lawn.

Horticulture Help Desk (Virginia Cooperative Extension)
www.fairfaxmastergardeners.org
    The horticulture help desk is staffed by master gardeners who will research your gardening questions and give you advice, both technical and practical. Contact by voice mail at 703-324-8556 or by e-mail at mgfairfax@vt.edu.

Northern Virginia Soil and Water Conservation District
www.fairfaxcounty.gov/NVSWCD
    Extensive information about preserving our watershed. Useful listserv. Quarterly Saturday "Green Breakfasts" open to the public on a wide variety of environmental subjects.

Plant Clinics (Virginia Cooperative Extension)
www.fairfaxmastergardeners.org
> Beginning in early May, members of the Fairfax County Cooperative Extension Master Gardeners host Plant Clinics. These Plant Clinics are held at various libraries and farmers markets.

Virginia Cooperative Extension www.ext.vt.edu
> Education, 4-H. Very extensive collection of tip sheets specific to gardening in Virginia.

Watershed calendar
> You can subscribe to periodic emails designed for volunteer stream monitors but which feature other local events as well such as native plants sales. There are two listservs, so during the signup, people should be sure to click on the Watershed Calendar and not the NEST listserve. www.fairfaxcounty.gov/NVSWCD

Societies

American Horticultural Society
> *American Gardener* magazine included with membership. River Farms garden. www.ahs.org

Arlington Rose Society
> Association of rose lovers www.arlingtonrose.org

Audubon at Home program
> Excellent practical information about gardening with native plants. Make your property an official "Wildlife Sanctuary." They also send ambassadors to your home to guide you through your landscaping choices. www.audubonva.org

Camellia Society of the Potomac Region
> Association of camellia lovers. http://cspv.org

Earth Sangha
Operates an ecological restoration program for the D.C. area to restore native forests and meadows, stabilize streams, and control invasive alien plants. Volunteer opportunities at wild plant nursery in Springfield, Meadowwood Recreation Area on Mason Neck, Native Arboretum in McLean, and others.   www.earthsangha.org

National Capital Area Garden Clubs, Inc.
An affiliation of 94 garden clubs
www.ncagardenclubs.org

National Capital Orchid Society
Association of orchid lovers   www.ncos.us/ncos/index.htm

Old Dominion Chrysanthemum Society
Association of chrysanthemum lovers   www.odcsmums.org

Virginia Native Plant Society
Excellent brochures on groundcovers, butterfly gardens, native alternatives, *etc.*. Newsletter.
www.vnps.org

Virginia Native Plant Society - Potomac Chapter
Local events, Yahoo group for announcements.
www.vnps-pot.org/home

Washington Daffodil Society
Association of daffodil lovers
www.washingtondaffodilsociety.org

Web sites

gardenweb.com   http://dir.gardenweb.com/directory
Directory of public gardens and clubs

Invasive.org
    Running list of invasive species.

Native alternatives to invasive aliens
    www.vnps.org/content/brochures
    www.usna.usda.gov/Gardens/faqs/InvasivesAlternatives.html

Rain garden web site
    www.fairfaxcounty.gov/nvswcd/raingarden.htm

YouGrowGirl.com
    Amusing commentary

Bee
Balm

Index

Student Peace Awards of Fairfax County

Starting in 2006, our group of sponsors has been offering awards to high school juniors and seniors who have made a contribution to peace or conflict resolution, whether in their schools, their communities, or the greater world. We started in one high school and have gradually expanded. Our goal is to offer it in each of the forty or so high schools in Fairfax County.

Our sponsors are non-profit organizations and faith communities, all of whom contribute $150 plus any volunteer assistance they are able to provide. We welcome others to join us.

Each high school is invited to design its own selection process. Examples of items to be considered include:
- Demonstrated commitment to peace by engaging in activities that strive to end conflict, either locally or globally.
- Demonstrated efforts to discuss or otherwise resolve potentially controversial issues within the school or community to bring about positive resolutions to those issues.
- Demonstrated efforts to promote the understanding of divisive issues and situations to bridge language, ethnic, racial, religious, gender, sexual orientation, or class differences.
- Demonstrated efforts to resolve conflicts among students or members of the community who feel isolated or alienated.

The students are notified of the award in early December. We hold a reception for them and their families in March and present them with their awards at their schools' honors ceremonies at the end of the academic year. Volunteers are always needed to present the awards, help with the reception, and assist with other tasks, none of which are very time consuming.

For more information, see www.herndonfriends.org/PeaceAwards, check out our Facebook page (which includes videos of keynote speeches at our receptions), or write c/o Herndon Friends Meeting, 660 Spring Street, Herndon, VA 20170. If you live outside of Fairfax County and would like to start a similar award in your own area, we would be happy to help with advice. We have put many of our basic documents on our web site to make it easier for others to get started.

CPSIA information can be obtained at www.ICGtesting.com
Printed in the USA
BVOW030035210312

285641BV00006B/4/P